MW01671979

Index

"HEY HEIST-OUT, NICE TRY BUT... LET'S TALK IN 100 YEARS"
europa star
ART & HOROLOGY
EMERGING BRANDS
heist out
Spring/Summer 2023
Issue 0
europa star
Since 1927, Europa Star is an international watch magazine published in over 170 countries. Don't forget to get every copy

no cap, only watches.
Patek o Plomo
hic & nunc

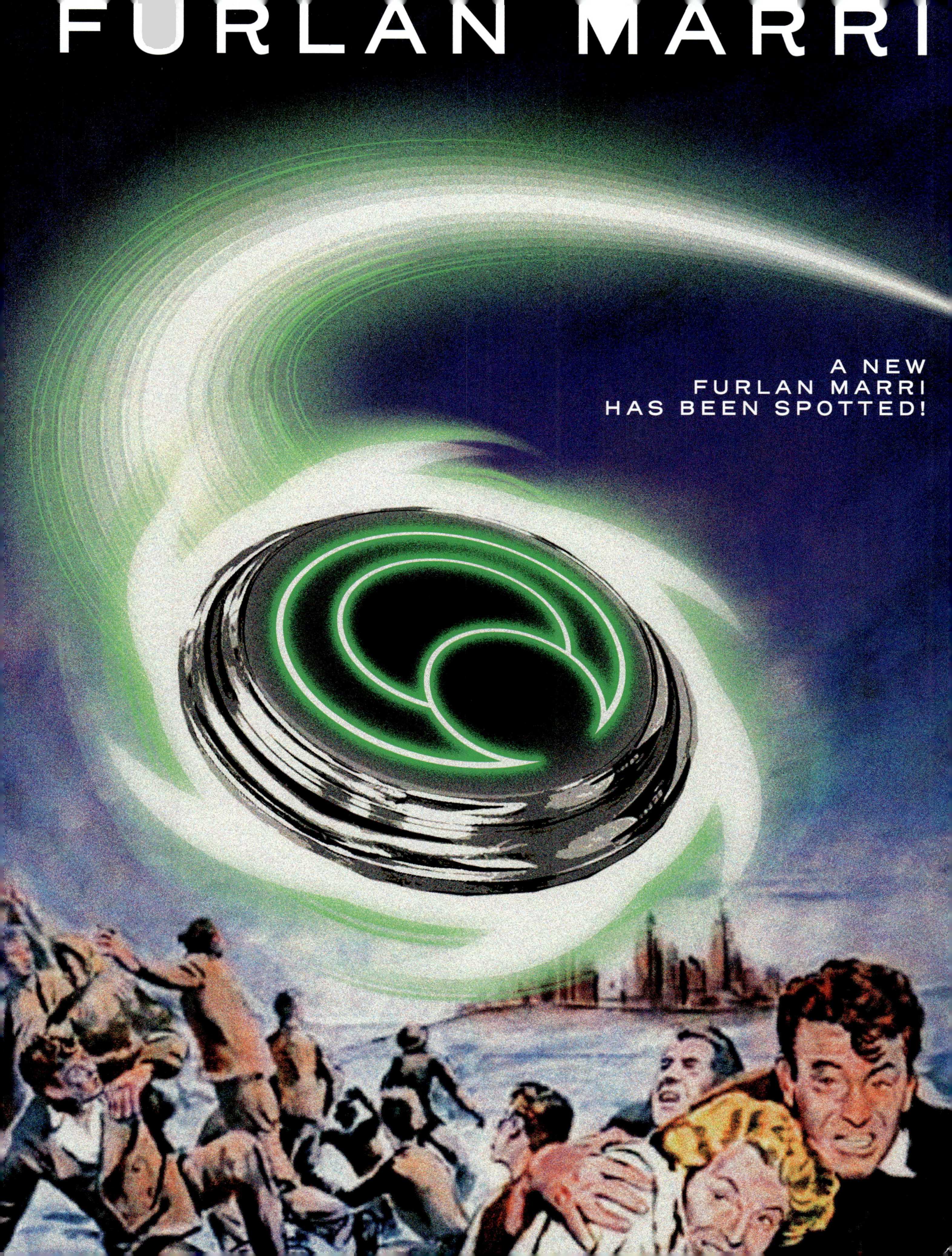
FURLAN MARRI
A NEW
FURLAN MARRI
HAS BEEN SPOTTED!

BACK TO SCHOOL

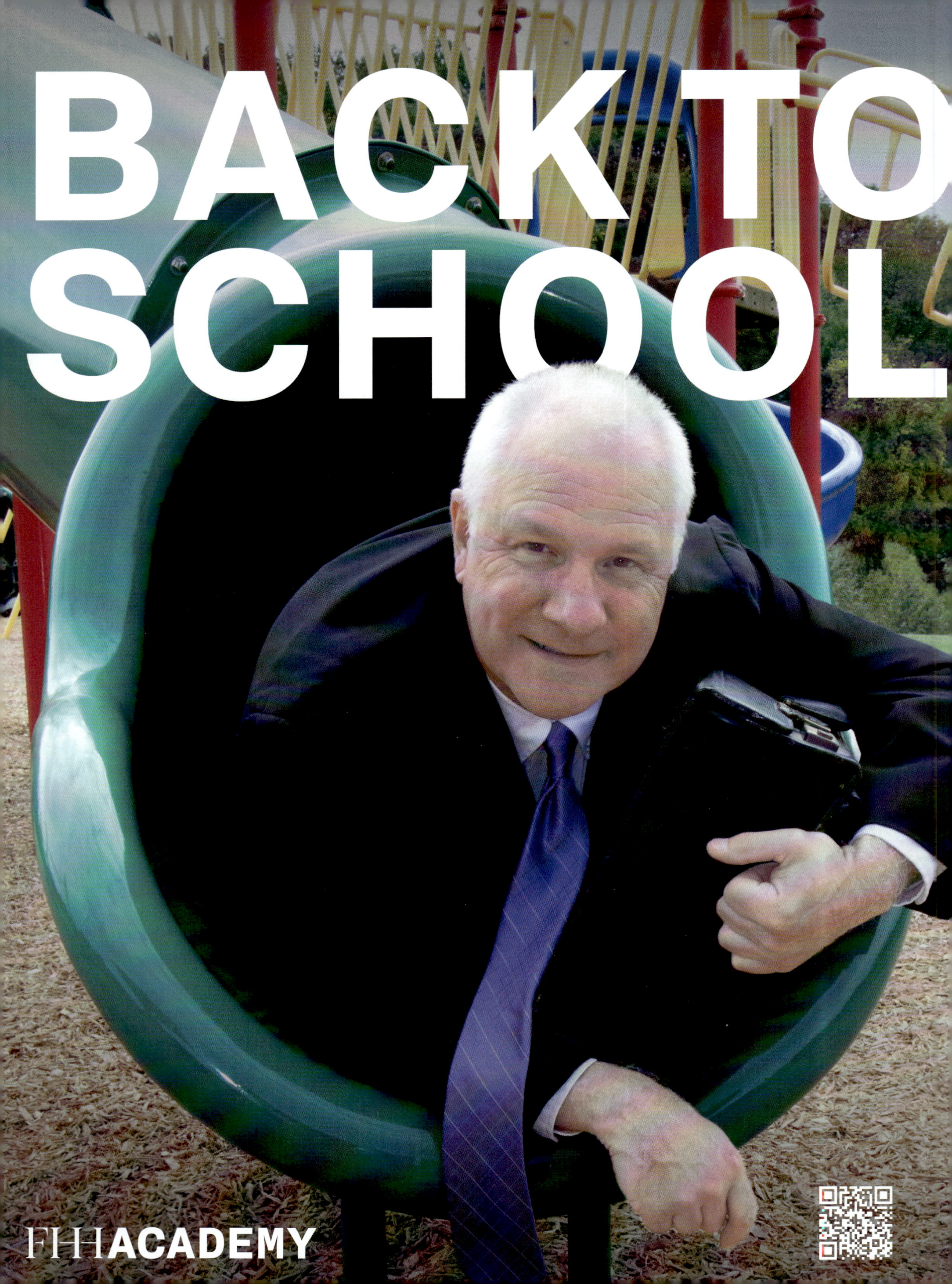

FHHACADEMY

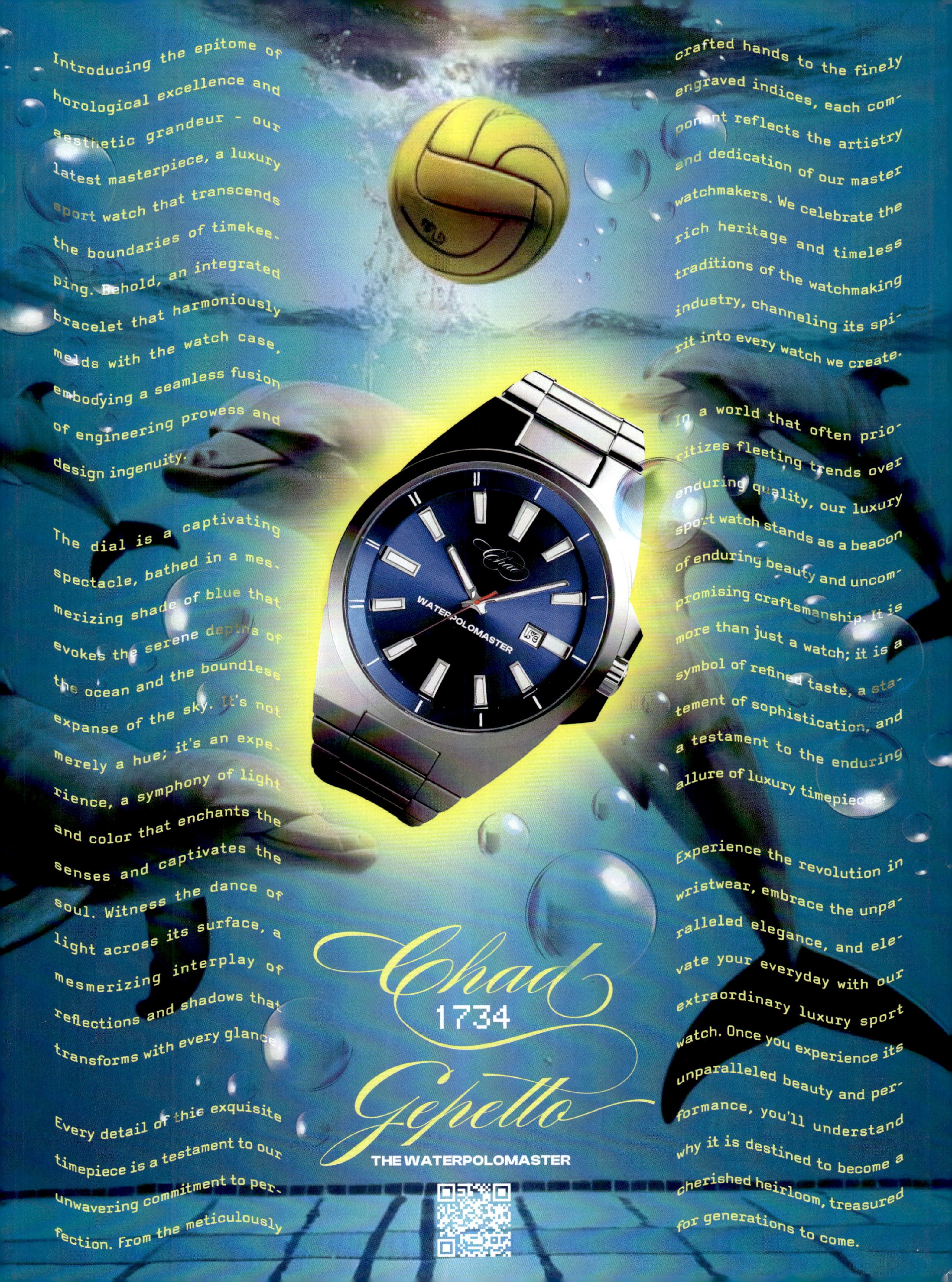
Introducing the epitome of horological excellence and aesthetic grandeur - our latest masterpiece, a luxury sport watch that transcends the boundaries of timekee-ping. Behold, an integrated bracelet that harmoniously melds with the watch case, embodying a seamless fusion of engineering prowess and design ingenuity.
The dial is a captivating spectacle, bathed in a mes-merizing shade of blue that evokes the serene depths of the ocean and the boundless expanse of the sky. It's not merely a hue; it's an expe-rience, a symphony of light and color that enchants the senses and captivates the soul. Witness the dance of light across its surface, a mesmerizing interplay of reflections and shadows that transforms with every glance.
Every detail of this exquisite timepiece is a testament to our unwavering commitment to per-fection. From the meticulously crafted hands to the finely engraved indices, each com-ponent reflects the artistry and dedication of our master watchmakers. We celebrate the rich heritage and timeless traditions of the watchmaking industry, channeling its spi-rit into every watch we create.
In a world that often prio-ritizes fleeting trends over enduring quality, our luxury sport watch stands as a beacon of enduring beauty and uncom-promising craftsmanship. It is more than just a watch; it is a symbol of refined taste, a sta-tement of sophistication, and a testament to the enduring allure of luxury timepieces.
Experience the revolution in wristwear, embrace the unpa-ralleled elegance, and ele-vate your everyday with our extraordinary luxury sport watch. Once you experience its unparalleled beauty and per-formance, you'll understand why it is destined to become a cherished heirloom, treasured for generations to come.
WATERPOLOMASTER
Chad
1734
Gepetto
THE WATERPOLOMASTER

STANDING THE TEST OF TIME

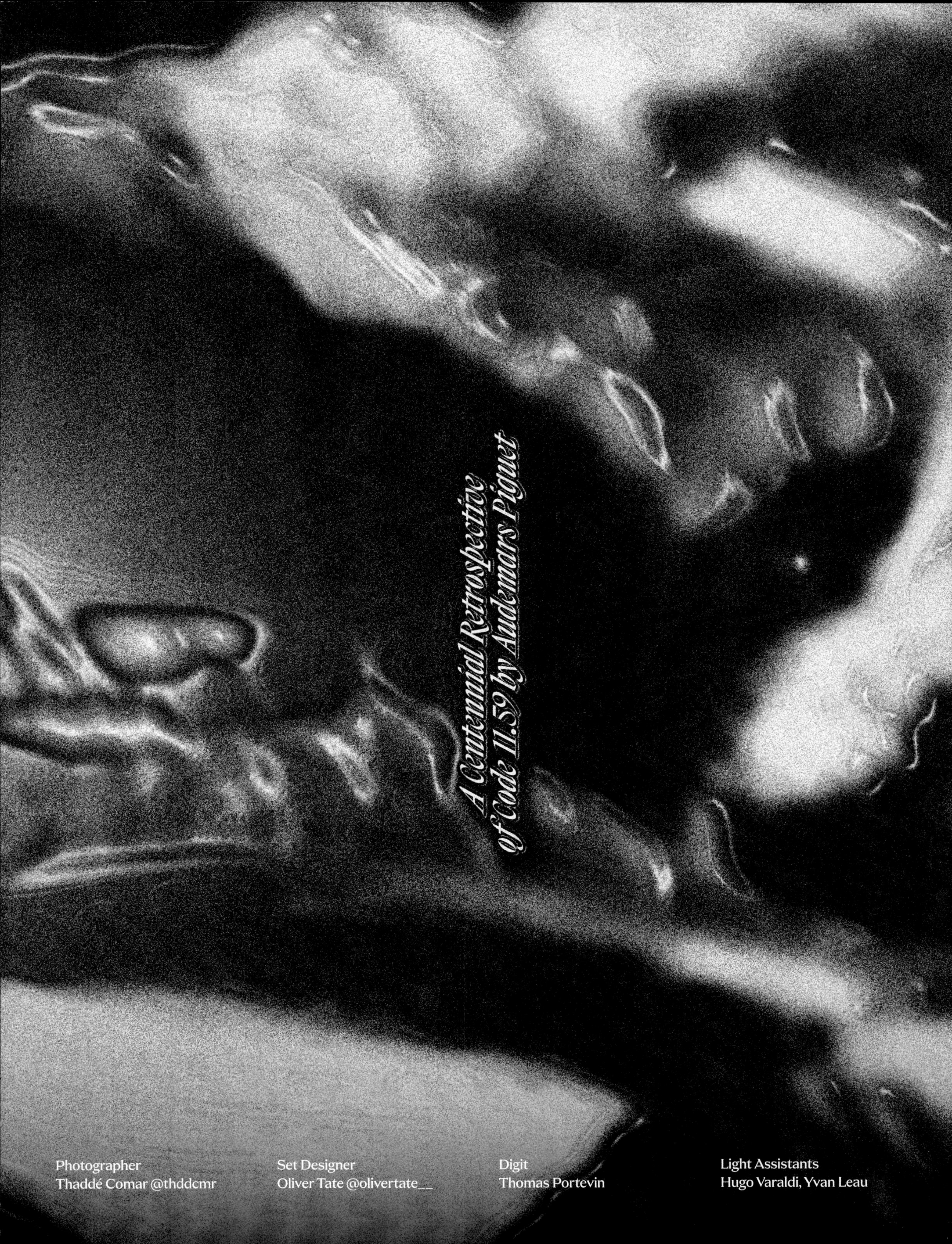

A Centennial Retrospective of Code 11.59 by Audemars Piguet

Photographer
Thaddé Comar @thddcmr

Set Designer
Oliver Tate @olivertate__

Digit
Thomas Portevin

Light Assistants
Hugo Varaldi, Yvan Leau

In the epoch of 2119, the landscape of our world has transformed immeasurably. Digital Electricity reigns supreme as the global currency, and automation has supplanted human effort in myriad sectors, watchmaking included — Yet, only a few actors remain steadfast, resisting the relentless advance of mechanization and placing their trust in the human touch.

Today, we celebrate the centennial of the Code 11.59 by Audemars Piguet, launched in 2019. This collection stands as a proof to enduring craftsmanship, seamlessly balancing tradition with modernity, and showcasing an unwavering commitment to design guided by the human eye and hand.

The Exhibition

Venture through time with us as we present a curated selection of iconic Code 11.59 by Audemars Piguet timepieces, introduced to the world a century ago. Each model encapsulates the essence of its era while maintaining the collection's distinctive aesthetic and spirit of innovation. These watches from another time have been artfully placed in a contemporary digital setting, accentuating their historical craftsmanship and meticulous attention to detail. It remains a testament to the intricate human artistry that continues to define the legacy of Code 11.59 by Audemars Piguet, up to this day.

Acknowledgements

We extend our sincere gratitude to Audemars Piguet's Heritage Department for generously loaning these century-old masterpieces from the Musée Atelier Audemars Piguet in Le Brassus.

Code 11.59 by Audemars Piguet
Selfwinding, 41mm, pink gold case

AUDEMARS PIGUET

Code 11.59 by Audemars Piguet
Selfwinding Chronograph, 41mm, pink gold case

Code 11.59 by Audemars Piguet
selfwinding, 38mm, pink gold case

AUDEMARS PIGUET
SWISS MADE

Code 11.59 by Audemars Piguet
Selfwinding Chronograph, 41mm, pink gold case

iced out

Julien Bon
Watch dealer and fashion collector
@julientoretto

Elias Marte
Watch collector and jewellery fanatic
@staycrispymyfriends

Heist-Out Can you recall the first time a watch on a hip-hop artist grabbed your attention?

Elias I grew up in the '90s with hip-hop as a constant. "Video Music Box" was my go-to early hip-hop channel, distinct from MTV, which was more mainstream. I remember seeing Tupac wearing Rolexes around '94-'95, making him the first rapper I saw with one. Biggie was also influenced by watches, it's clear from the references in his music and visuals. Tupac consistently showcased his Rolexes, even in movies, setting him apart from other rappers. Speaking about this you can find here the receipt of his the first Rolex he bought in 1993.

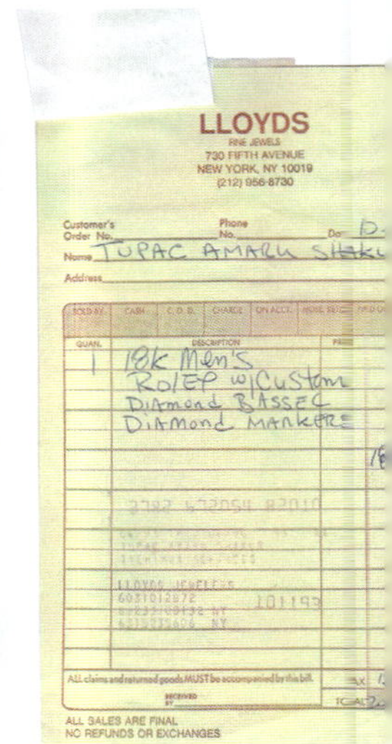
LLOYDS
FINE JEWELS
730 FIFTH AVENUE
NEW YORK, NY 10019
(212) 956-8730

Customer's Order No. Phone No.
Name TUPAC AMARU SHAK
Address

QUAN.	DESCRIPTION
1	18k Men's Rolex w/Custom Diamond Bassel Diamond Markers

ALL claims and returned goods MUST be accompanied by this bill.
RECEIVED BY
ALL SALES ARE FINAL
NO REFUNDS OR EXCHANGES

Julien For me, Nas stood out with the Rolex on "Stillmatic" cover. I admired the colours, his velvet tracksuit, and the watch, likely a Day-Date Pearlmaster. But if you ask me, this is a shitty-looking bracelet.

HO What's your earliest watch and hip-hop memory?

J I recall seeing LL Cool J in "The Source" magazine with a Credor or a Seiko Gold Nugget. Unsure if it was custom or factory-made. I actually found a pretty similar model, a gold-plated Seiko, and I remember flexing with it! *laughs*.

E Big Tymers in '98-'99 stood out for me, especially as a car enthusiast. Playing Gran Turismo 1 and 2, I resonated with their car talk. They flaunted Rolexes, stylish medallions, and Yokohama tyres. I recall a video where they rocked two watches simultaneously. Growing up in New York, rappers often drove Mercedes Benz and Lexus. The Big Timers, however, rolled in Jaguars, limos, and Hummers—taking it to the next level.

HO When did wristwear become the ultimate ego flex in hip-hop? Who excelled most in this trend, and who do you believe pioneered it?

J Hip-hop thrives on competition: the best lyrics, style, and accessories. From the start, it's been about who rocks the biggest chain or the priciest watch. I believe it's been part of the culture since the beginning. Run-DMC popularised big chains and watches. Eric B & Rakim sported a watch similar to LL Cool J's Golden Nugget piece. Slick Rick stood out with his wild style, custom Rolexes, and extravagant chains.

E For me, Slick Rick stands out. The pivotal moment for hip-hop and watches was Eric B and Rakim with their iconic roll chains in the late '80s. While Slick Rick wasn't a watch aficionado, he rocked watches as bling, setting the trend for '90s rappers to emulate.

HO What ignited the ego-trip trend in rap music? Any insights?

E It's about flaunting success. Beyond rapping skills, rappers showcase achievements in various domains. Alongside hip-hop's four essential elements, breakdance, deejay, graffiti, and rapping, I'd add style as the fifth. It's a competitive arena where displaying financial well-being is key. Once you start earning, splurging becomes tempting, especially if you couldn't afford it before.

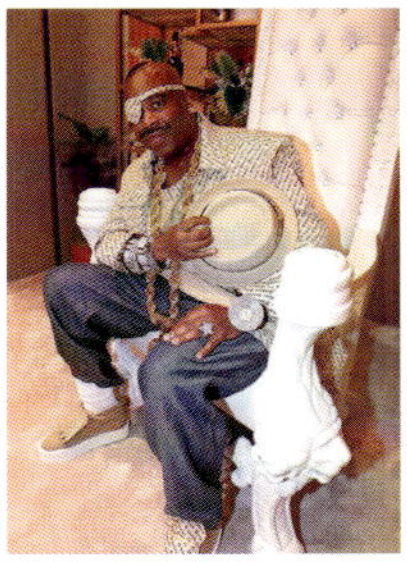

HO Do you believe some were putting on a facade?

E Not necessarily faking it, but some borrowed watches initially. Take Nas, for instance. In '94/'95, before his success, he borrowed a friend's old Day-Date. He persuaded his manager, Steve Style, to buy one to appear more credible in meetings. Wearing imitation jewellery or watches is also part of the "fake it till you make it" ethos.

HO What's the most memorable flex from that era?

E To me, the "Wu" logo on a Rolex Day-Date stands out. Icing out a watch is one thing, but customising the dial with the "Wu" logo is next-level and iconic. It stands among my top custom watch designs. Wu-Tang's influence is truly inspirational.

J I agree. It's the most impactful one.

HO Do you know who currently owns that watch? Is it still a member of the Wu-Tang Clan?

J I believe it's Raekwon. I recently saw a podcast interview in which he seemed to wear it.

HO What's the grail watch for rappers?

E I'd say it's likely a Rolex Day-Date or Datejust. It's the entry point, and then you climb the ladder to brands like AP and Patek.

J Absolutely. You can almost always spot a rapper with a Datejust or Day-Date.

HO Is it still the go-to choice for newcomers, even today?

E Yes, many are returning to classic watches.

J When Gucci Mane signs newcomers, he gifts them a custom Datejust or Day-Date as a team welcome.

HO Like us, they often start with Rolex when they can afford it, move away, and eventually come back to it.

J That's the circle.

HO Do you have any iconic watch-related lyrics that come to mind?

E Um, I believe Raekwon was the first rapper to mention Vacheron Constantin in a rap song in 1999. He's one of the top five best-dressed rappers. It's impressive that he had that watch knowledge in '99 when most stores shunned rappers. Nowadays, with stylists and online resources, it's easier to gain watch knowledge. But back then, mentioning VC showed genuine expertise.

J Recently, at the gym, I heard Jadakiss joke about stealing watches in clubs.

HO Before Adidas collaborated with Run-DMC, many brands overlooked or even dismissed rappers. How did they still gravitate towards watches? Are there any notable references, intriguing facts, or iconic lyrics that highlight this?

E Interesting fact: Hip-hop is the genre that most pro-minently showcases watches. While many might not admit it, no other genre mentions watches more than rap. Swatch was among the first brands to engage with hip-hop through "The Fat Boys commercial." Their strategy targeted demographics and aimed to penetrate the US market. Check it out on YouTube; it's remarkable and predates the Adidas-Run DMC partnership.

HO Interestingly, it was one of the more affordable brands to first target the hip-hop industry.

E Yeah, terms like "busted downs," "high style", "iced-out", and "Rollie" originated from hip-hop. Brands now use these expressions in ads, and "bling bling" is even in the US dictionary. Despite initial resistance, hip-hop undeniably influences.

HO As you mentioned, brands initially denied them access, so they resorted to buying on the secondary market.

J It's a love-hate relationship. Luxury brands once shunned hip-hop culture, but things are slowly changing for the better.

"had the whole block
locked selling tons in Morocco,
wristwatch,
Vacheron Constantin."

"Never will it stop,
handguns
with double-digit shots
I move work
on other niggas blocks
Leave out the club
with another niggas watch
Body that man
and let other nigga watch"

HO What prompted rappers to customise their watches, and why did they choose diamonds?

J Back then, customisation was essential. Like Dapper Dan with Louis Vuitton, it's about having something unique. Owning a Rolex isn't enough; it's having one with diamonds. It's about standing out, flexing, and engaging in visible competition.

E In the '90s, watch customisation became an extension of jewellery. Many rappers replaced the original dial without a second thought. By the 2000s, jewellery and watches had to match together. Rappers like Prodigy and Mobb Deep even coordinated chains with their watches. Tito's sister (more on this later on) mentioned that because of their wealth, rappers didn't worry about resale or versatility. If they needed another piece, they simply bought a new one. Nas's photo exemplifies this. After getting a massive "Queensbridge" chain, he got a matching Rolex by Tito Caceido. It's like saying, "I have a big chain, so now I need the big watch."

HO Are rappers interested in watch complications?

J Yeah, Jay-Z is definitely into it. He's likely the most prominent collector and among the first to show interest in complications.

E Jay-Z, definitely. Always wanting to be the first, he's evolved over the years and seeks recognition. In the 2000s, with a clothing line, acquisitions, and a personal plane, he'd likely flex with something like, "I'm crossing time zones post-concert, so I rely on my Jacob 'Five Time Zone' to keep track."

HO Who is the Dapper Dan of watches and jewellery, and who's your favourite? What's the most impressive piece you've seen?

E For me, it's Tito. He pioneered bust downs and custom pieces like no one else. While Jacob rose to prominence later, many stayed loyal to Tito before shifting allegiances.

J It's Jacob with the Five Time Zone watch, even if it's a bit ugly *laughs*. I remember playing Def Jam on my PlayStation 2, and Jacob was in the game.

HO Is the "Five Time Zone" a must-have in the hip-hop game?

J Everyone was wearing it, from Jay-Z to Paris Hilton and many more. I remember searching eBay for one. Despite many fakes, I got one.

HO Do you have any amusing stories about watch-related disrespect due to customisation?

E I'd say the "Imaginary Players" beef between Jay-Z and Mase. It all started when Jay-Z dissed Mase in the song: "Where's all the ice with all the platinum under that? Those ain't Rolex diamonds, what the fuck you done to that?". He was referring to Mase's new bussed-down Rolex, which he had bought from Jacob. Mase took it personally and replied, "Platinum this, platinum that, you talk about platinum, but you don't have any platinum hits". Let's put it in context: in the '90s, Mase was way bigger than Jay-Z. "Reasonable doubt" is a classic to us, but it didn't sell so well back then. He teases him, suggesting he buys a platinum watch to compensate for non-platinum hits. "Imaginary Players" subtly disses custom, and while it's a popular song, many don't realise it targeted Mase over a watch. Now you know.

J The Virgil Abloh customised Patek Philippe Nautilus 5726 with the all-black PVD stands out. While I don't oppose customisation, it feels a bit disrespectful to watchmakers who meticulously craft these watches, especially with many intricate features. You've got a f*cking moon phase complication, and you plunge it in plastic.

HO Who did the modification?

J I think it's MAD Paris. But I'm not sure. I know they did Drake's Patek, though.

HO The one with the emeralds?

J Yeah, the worst setting ever... *laughs*

HO What's the current state of the watch game in hip-hop? Has it evolved?

E Drake mixes vintage with new buys. Jay-Z's unpredictable, switching between bust down and complex timepieces. Pharrell sets trends, from diamond-studded Casios to Richard Mille UP-01. Rihanna rocks a custom King Midas. Among the new gen, 42 Dugg chats about Pateks and APs, both blinged-out and classic. He's always adding to his collection, "Oh, I just came out from jail. I wanna buy the 5900" *laughs*.

HO Are the principles still the same: bust down, big names, complications, customs?

E Some are reverting to plain Jane. I'd mention N.O.R.E, who hosts a podcast and was into bust downs in the 2000s. He's a big watch enthusiast with a longstanding watch career; my friends even interviewed him. Shoutout to his crew. Now, he's diversifying his collection. I've spotted him at watch events and clubs buying plain Jane pieces. I saw him eyeing a Horace Watts at a club once, eager to purchase. He was like, "Oh my God, can I buy today?".

J I admire Gucci Man's collection. Many rappers shout him out when discussing watches or chains. He buys both factory and non-factory pieces, which is fine by me.

HO In other industries, collabs with rappers are a big deal. Are they legitimate in the watch industry as well?

J No, but the AP collaborations with Travis and Alix stands out. Whether you like it or not, the execution was solid. The communication design had a clear concept, and the whole package was spot-on, in my opinion.

E I won't comment on collaborations, but hip-hop's influence on the watch game is significant. Hodinkee notices Jay-Z's new watch courtside at NBA games, and people discuss the yet-to-be-released RM that Pharrell wears.

HO How would you want watches to mix with the hip-hop scene in the future? What do you want to see that hasn't been done or that could shake up the watch realm?

J I like it the way it is now. I don't want to see everybody doing huge collabs with watch brands. I don't want any MoonSwatch vibes, either.

E I agree with Julien. I'm content with how it is right now. It must feel authentic.

HO Can we finish with our infamous "What's one thing you'd like to share to conclude this interview that you never imagined would make it into a magazine?"

E It always originates from the streets. That's why Mike Tyson is one of my favourite athletes; he's always embodied that street essence. He maintained connections to the streets while pursuing boxing as his career. I believe trends often stem from the streets.

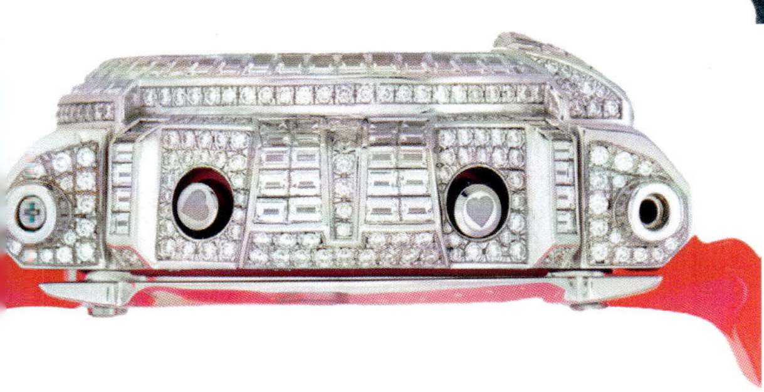

HO Julien, you already laid it down in our last issue, but got anything else you wanna drop?

J I need to go to the gym.

HO Haha, that's a good one! *laughs* Nobody would care. Thanks again, peace out.

Rejjie Snow
@rejjiesnow

Arthur Pfister
@arthuroduro

Stacking

Alex, aka Rejjie Snow, is a 30-year-old multi-disciplinary artist who first made waves with his music. Born & raised in Dublin City, in the Concrete Jungle, he moved to the U.S. at 18 with a football scholarship while studying art. It was during this time that Alex dipped his toes into the music scene, sharing his beats on SoundCloud. At 20, he returned to his home country to pursue his music career. Discovering different creative spaces through music, he started designing clothing, jewellery, and painting and is now experimenting with designing watches. His newfound love for horology is what brought us together, and I, Arthur Pfister, feel privileged to chat with him and delve into his perspectives on the world of watches.

Photographer
Lara Shapiro @ljshapiro

A What was your first passion?

RJ Number one was Football. Every day from 5 years old. I really wanted to become a professional football player, but I realised I was missing the extra 10%. But no doubt, this was my first passion. I've lost that passion a little, I feel like there's too much money in Football, and I feel like players give only 50% of themselves. The second one right behind is graffiti. I still do it. The adrenaline, there's nothing like it. It feels almost meditative and therapeutic.

A Who inspired you as a teenager? Who inspires you now?

RJ My father and Pharrell Williams. When I saw him, I was like, 'I wanna be you.' For sure. Now, my daughter inspires me. When you get older, you see people for who they are, and they get more humanised, so naturally, she's my first inspiration because she gives me 100% every day. Motivation. She is three years old now. And highly capable.

A How do you balance your time between exploring/working your diverse professions (music, art, design) and how do you stay creative while working?

RJ Honestly, it's not easy, it's really hard. I think, for us, no one feels sorry for us so we just have to keep going. On my side, I try to exercise, eat well, so when I do feel down, I'm not totally down, full crash. I'm able to get back up, take the punches and go with the flow. So yeah, I'm prioritising health really. Creatively speaking, it all comes naturally to me. When I get ideas, it's almost like not me, I'm not forcing anything, not thinking too much, it just comes from somewhere. Even with the lyrics, most of the time I do it in my head and then I go to the studio. I usually work in L.A. for this, as most of my producers work there.

A Do you have a memory of the first watch you saw/loved, where you felt something?

RJ Rolex. All my family owned Rolex models. They always had nice watches. I can remember the first time they told me it was a Rolex, and I had one in my hand. I can still picture the crown on the dial. I'll never forget it. Rolex is big in Dublin, more than any other watch brand.

A What's your relationship with vintage?

RJ In clothing, I've always liked stuff that was closer to the original, things that now bring me nostalgia. It all started when I was 16 years old with graffiti. I loved '70s and '80s graffiti styles, so I was naturally exposed to old-school. It all came together with clothing and hip-hop music. From that point, it was diamonds, bling, Jacob & Co, and that's how I got exposed to watch culture. All custom stuff. It didn't matter if it lost its value, it was all about the image in hip-hop.

A How did you get into watches? How did your collecting style develop?

RJ It started off late for me. Once I began making a bit of money from music, I started

"I also feel that with vintage, I can wear them every day, especially in London, it's more inconspicuous than a big flashy modern watch. Those just stand out too much"

buying watches because I thought that was what I was supposed to do. But I didn't know anything about watches or why and I never used to wear any. There was no passion, so it was almost like this awkward thing that you must wear on stage or whatever. I never really knew what to wear because there was no love involved. So I had like three or four watches, all Rolex. The passion came only 4 years ago. Being into watches for real, understanding how they're made, the vintage, the craftmanship, factory or custom-made, everything behind it. And now I get it. My first watch was an '80s Rolex Day-Date with a diamond dial and ruby indexes. Now that I've been more exposed to watches, I just choose what I like. If it's vintage, so be it, but I just have to love it. My wrist is small, though, so vintage is naturally more appealing. Another of my preferred watches is this Rolex Submariner double signed with Tiffany and Co. My style developed from 'Bust downs' to stainless steel pieces, diamond factory watches, vintage and neo-vintage pieces just recently. I love Gérald Genta's work from the '80s and '90s, very avant-garde and full of shapes. The size is great, it looks great with how I dress, and the variety of the brand is unmatched. I also feel that with vintage, I can wear them every day, especially in London, it's more inconspicuous than a big flashy modern watch. Those just stand out too much.

A Have you ever considered incorporating your passion for vintage watches into your music/art, either thematically or aesthetically?
RJ Never, but I always keep thinking about it, but then I'm always like, 'I have nothing to say that's too much of a flex'. I don't have a million-dollar watch. I did it recently in my new album. It's coming out next year. Lots of singles before that. If any watch brands want to work with me with the new album coming out, hit me up. I usually only work with fashion, but I would love to get into the watch culture, that'd be fun.

A You're a creator, an artist, a painter, a musician and a singer. What do you look for in a watch? Do you have a specific approach? Do you see the watch as a pure accessory, or do you connect to it on a deeper level?
RJ Character and value. Is it 18k gold? What are the stones worth? Is it factory-made? How many were made? I feel like real value is important in jewellery and watches. I see watches as pure accessories. I don't know if it's because we look at our phones all day now, but it's just the way it is. It's a reflection of the times we live in, to be honest.Although I have some watches in my collection that have become more symbolic through living and going through experiences with me. Some watches I just wear for people to be like 'Oh, you have this' and you know, just to flex. I feel like it's a very human feeling to want to flex something you worked hard for. Especially now that I'm working on designing my own watch.

A Is there a watch-acquiring moment that really sticks out in your memory?
RJ At the Cartier store in London. It was my first time buying a watch at an official retail shop. I bought a Cartier Tank Française there, and it was nice because my girl was with me. Most people buy on the grey market, and I think it's a shame.

A What's the best advice you've been given and the best advice you've given to yourself?
RJ The best advice I've been given was to learn something about everything, and everything about something. I've always told myself to dream big.

A Any last words?
RJ Stay dangerous.

As our conversation wound down, we touched upon the luxury of time. The devotion to one's craft is often understated. People are often in a rush to release their music. Yet, it takes time to understand your sound as an artist, and even if there's a temptation to compete with the most popular stuff going on, working on your craft will set you apart, proving invaluable in a long-term perspective. Naturally, you gotta have the luxury of time to do that. This applies to the watch industry and the newcomers on the market. Food for thought. Thank you, Alex, for taking the time.

Flash Questions

A Favourite movie?
RJ A Bronx Tale directed by Robert de Niro in 1993.

A Favourite artist?
RJ MF DOOM.

A Favourite holiday destination?
RJ Jamaïca.

A Unpopular opinion?
RJ I think it's ok to only like one or two songs from different artists. Liking a song shouldn't commit me to their whole discography or their personal life.

A One watch brand for modern?
RJ Patek.

A One watch brand for vintage?
RJ Audemars Piguet.

A Design your own Royal Oak?
RJ Stainless Steel, Quartz, Lapis Lazuli.

A Any brand novelties you looking forward to for 2024?
RJ Rolex.

Rolex King Midas, Coral stone dial

Vacheron Constantin

PRINT

Art Director & Photographer
Aydran Ryan Cook @beenstaying

Stylists
Sofija Zarubica @sofijazza
Hristijan Zhezhovski @zezotgod

Models
Assan Sowe @mrassansowe
Lea Krummenacher @leavocado
Ntokozo Joy mashiya @et3rnal_4rsOn_
Lea Molinnus @lizzymakesudizzy
Yannick Gross @yenne96

Watches
N°1 @yonikrissi
N°2 @lorenzo.maillard
N°3 @agm.1675
N°4 @hicnuncwatches
N°5 @thelazywatch

Jean Paul Gaultier
Looks 2, 4

Medieval Armor
Theater House Basel
Selva Meyer @venuscyborg

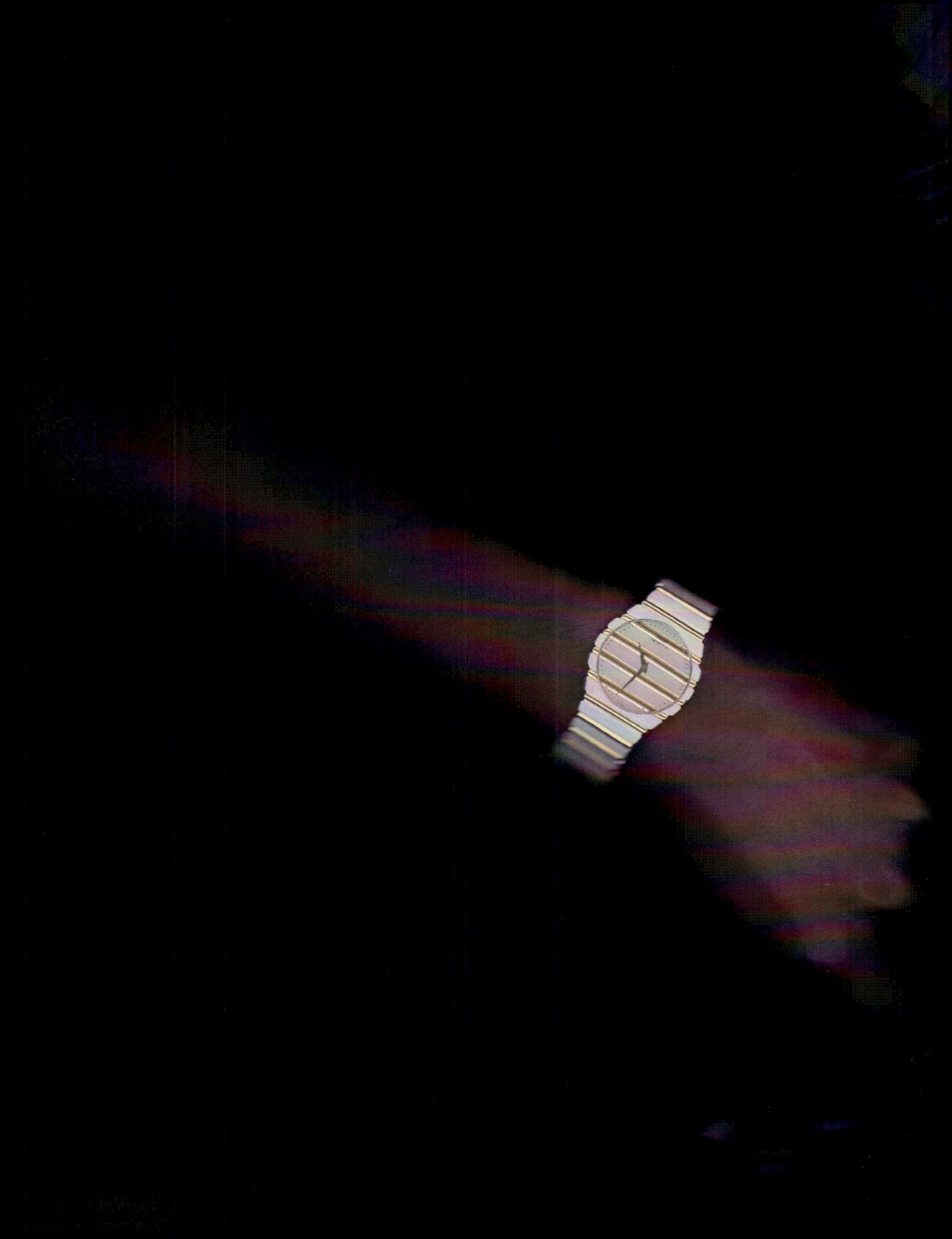

Piaget Polo

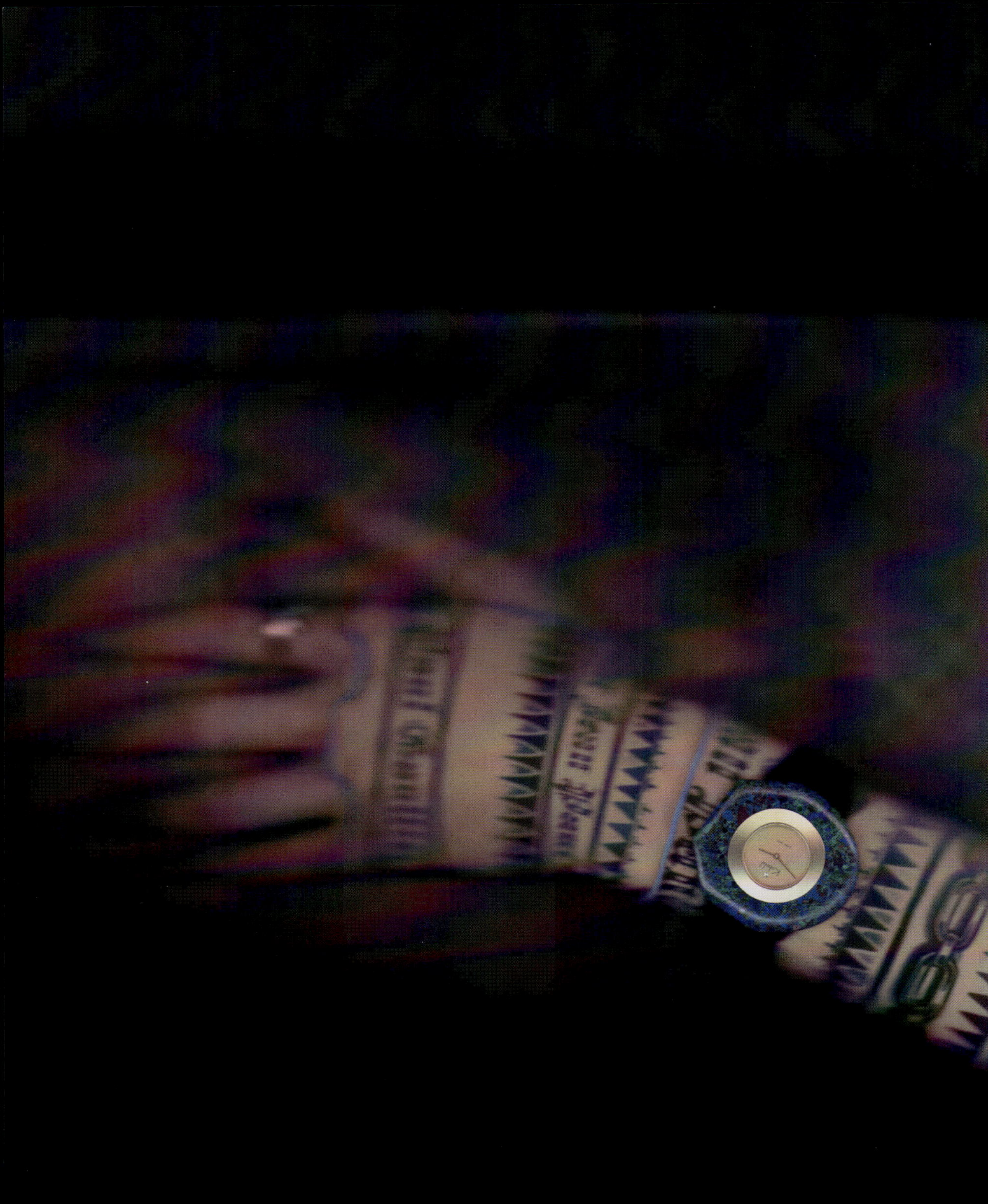

Kobold by Pierre M.

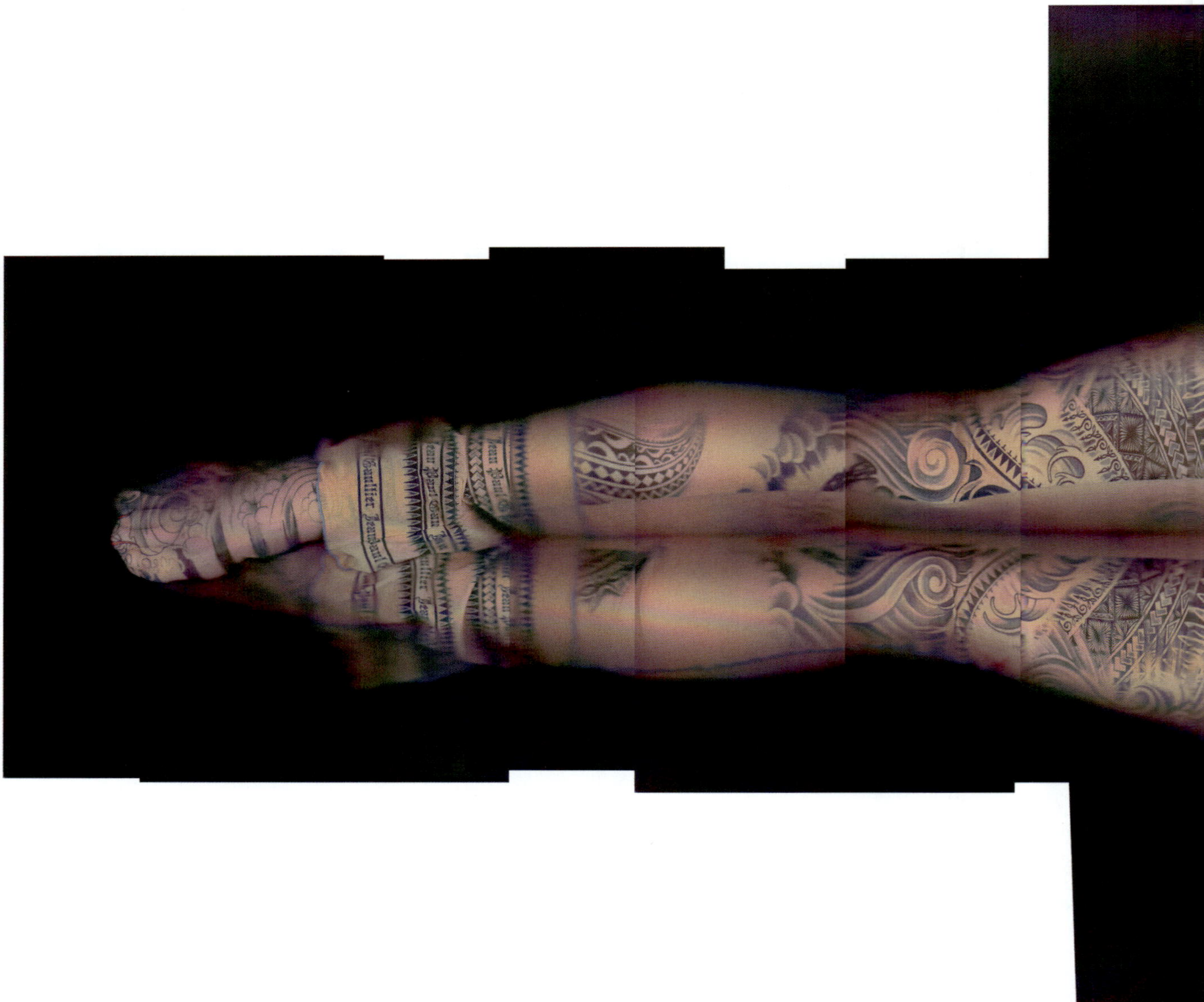

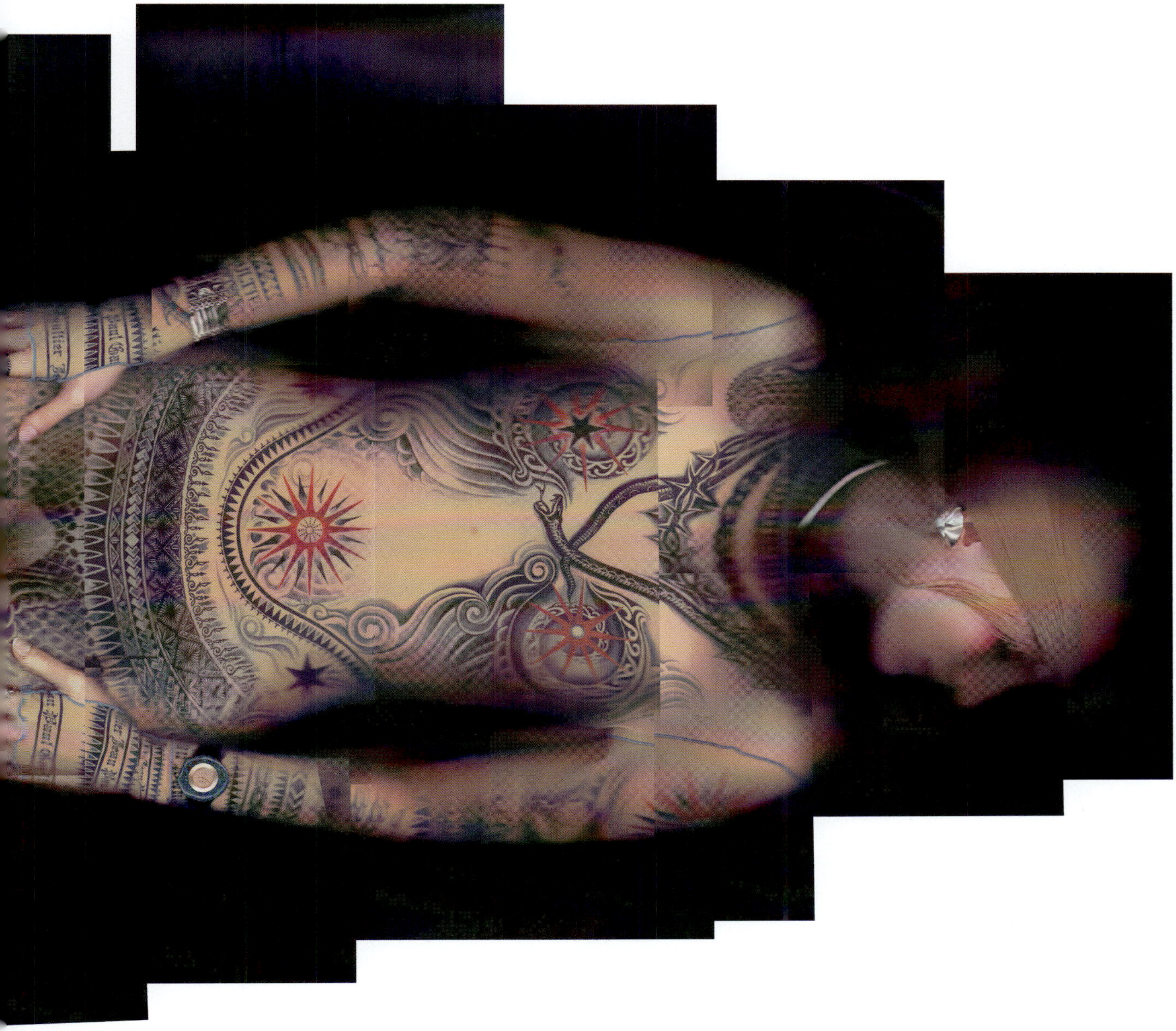

Rolex Day-Date

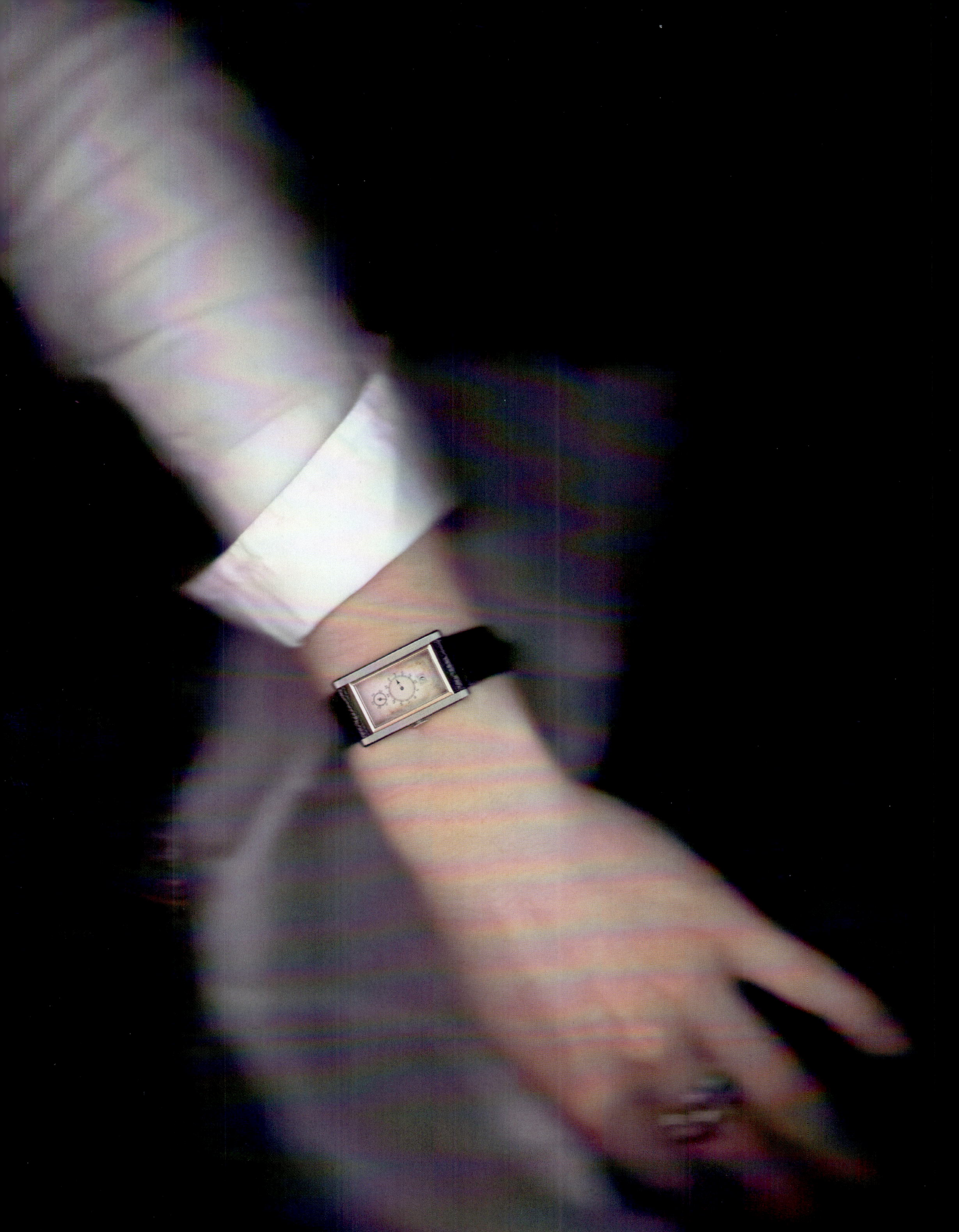

Niton Jumping Hours

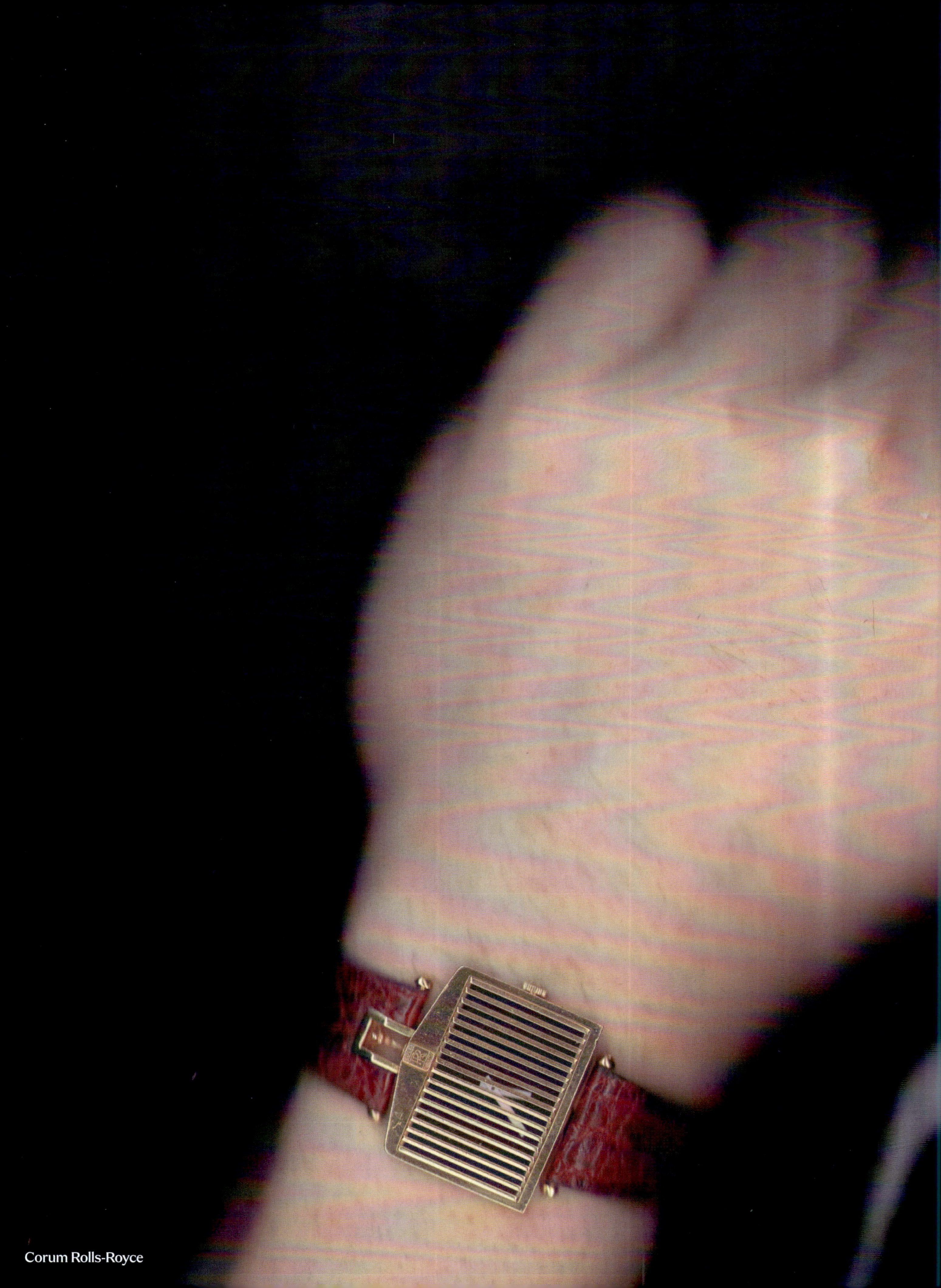

Corum Rolls-Royce

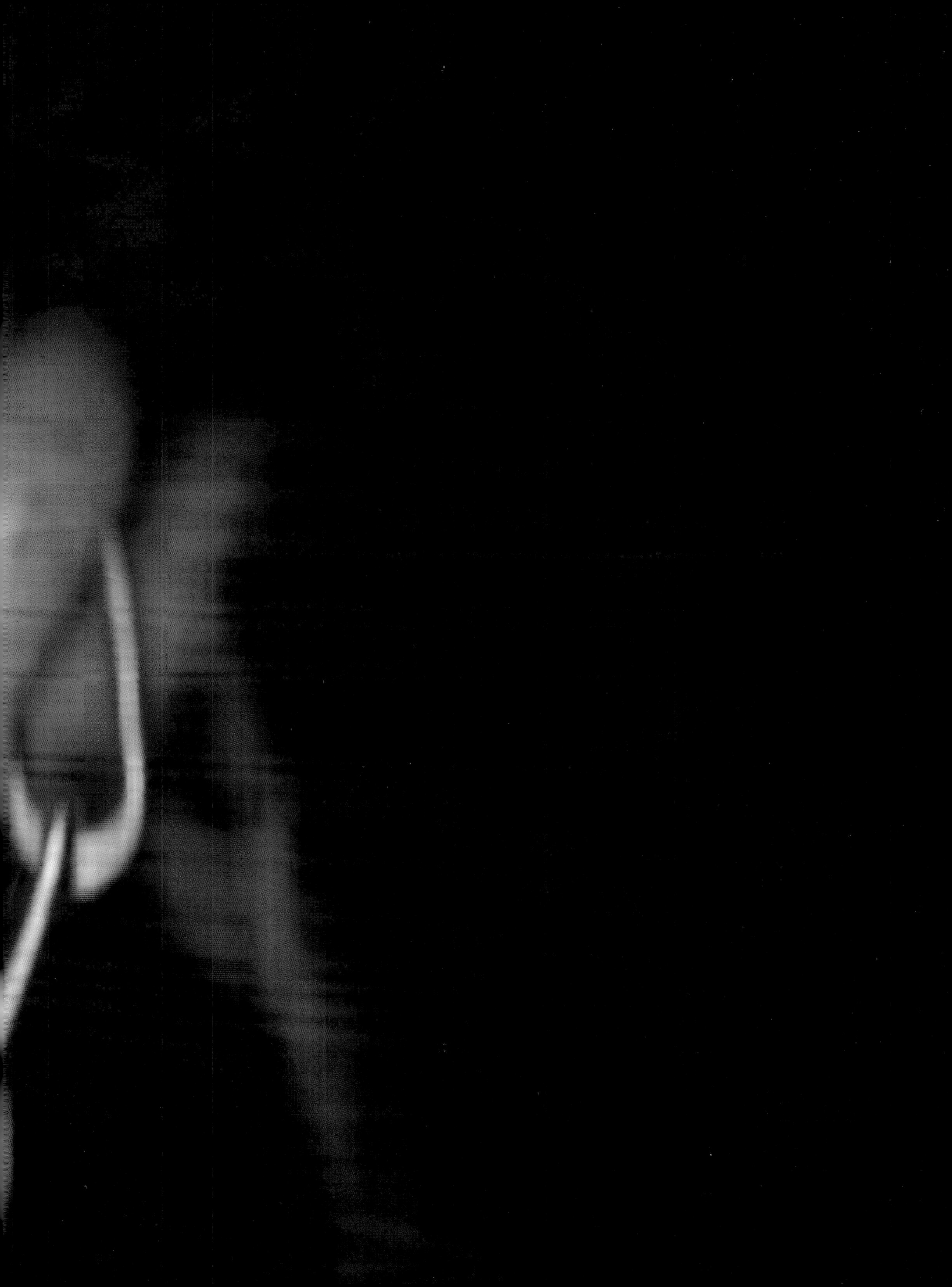

The B/1

Creating something is hard. And creating something new and different seems to be largely impossible. Whether we look at music—which today is very much influenced by jazz concocted several decades ago—, movies, fashion (which repeats itself in endless cycles) and, of course, horology. Most watches we see today are, in one way or another, influenced by the "Golden Era" of watchmaking that roughly took place between the 1950s and the 1970s, when designs were wild, bold, and unique. (And one could argue they were out of place when they came about.) Again, most of what we see today tends to look similar to what we've seen before! So, what would motivate anyone to create a watch brand in 2024? Or, precisely, embark on this project three years back and spend all that time refining a horological vision in secret? Well, this seems to stem from the desire to create

something that has never been seen before and which is, perhaps to everybody's surprise, still possible to achieve today. It takes a certain type of person to come up with a horological project that is both different and, at the same time, seems to come straight from the golden era of watchmaking we just mentioned. More specifically, it takes a multimedia, multi-dimensional artist and an unexpected—and a truly 21st-century—type of virtual connection to make this happen! But before we delve into horology, let's take a detour to meet Phillip Toledano, the co-creator and driving force behind the Toledano & Chan project. Born to a French Moroccan mother and American father, Toledano spent nearly two decades working in the bustling and ultra-competitive world of advertising in New York City. He graduated with a BA in literature from Tufts University in Boston, so you can imagine that Toledano must have had a special talent—or a set of skills—to cut his teeth on marketing. As he simply put it during our interview, anything starts with an idea. His experience in advertising enabled his creative mind to adapt to any idea he had. First comes the idea, and then comes the execution. Always.

by Toledano & Chan

Interviewed by Vincent Deschamps

This is evident when looking at his eclectic artistic portfolio: photography, videography, mixed media, writing, and now AI-generated collages. Toledano has consistently adapted his ideas to the new mediums available to him, or rather, new technologies and artistic trends have expanded his creativity and inspired him to dig into new themes. Whether he is documenting his father's life (after the sudden passing of his mother) in "Days With My Father" or exploring the strict ban of female figures on product packaging in the Middle East in his series "Abstent Portrait", Toledano has a unique approach to life, starting with an idea and then figuring out how to execute it.

For thousands of years, artists have been deeply influenced by their environment, as evidenced by the prehistoric cave paintings in France depicting local flora and fauna, as well as modern and contemporary art reflecting current political, social, and economic contexts. This is, in a nutshell, where Phillip Toledano drew inspiration when he started working on the first Toledano & Chan B/1 model. Living in New York City, Toledano was captivated by 1970s brutalist architecture and the bold watches designed by iconic designers like Gérald Genta and Jorg Hysek from the same era.

In all of his work prior to Toledano & Chan, Phillip has always been drawn to reinterpreting what he sees, reimagining what has been created before but from his personal, contemporary perspective. It's about reallocating the meaning of a type of art and, most importantly, adapting its original message to a new world. This concept is central to all he has done in recent years and how he approached his latest project: the B/1.

The B/1 is the embodiment of his design philosophy: translating brutalist architecture into watches, retelling the story of 1960s New York, and making it into a pragmatic, wearable, and relatively attainable piece of horology. As an adopted New Yorker, Toledano has been subtly inspired by the art and architecture of this majestic city. Having lived a few years there myself, I can attest to the endless inspiration one can find in the Big Apple. Many creatives who have settled there share one thing in common: they have unique ideas and want to contribute something different to the world. (I'm extrapolating a little bit here based on my personal experiences.)

However, the B/1 is not Toledano's sole doing. A few years back, although he can't remember how, he met Alfred Chan, a Hong Kong-based watch designer, online through Instagram. (A funny detail is that the two have yet to meet in the flesh.) They both shared an interest in brutalist architecture, and early in their online exchanges, neither imagined they would eventually create a watch brand. But one day, one fateful day, Todelano sent Chan a picture of a window from the Breuer building (the original home of the Whitney Museum of American Art), and they immediately knew this would be their first joint project: a sculptural watch that looks unique and remains attainable. (Yes, I promise to discuss the B/1 price in a bit.) Inspired by the sculptural aspect of 1970s watches like the Patek Philippe Nautilus and Rolex's King Midas, the B/1 is an honest testament to a slice of New York City's history and to watches which, as Toledano explains, constituted a complete artistic vision. It was a time when a few designers saw watches as whole entities and not just as interesting dials or case shapes. Where the case, dial, and bracelet seamlessly merge to create a comprehensive sculpture. As he put it, in any artistic project, "the concept must run throughout the entire idea." This is apparent in how Toledano and Chan designed each aspect of the B/1—from the dramatic flat and angular surfaces and the alternation of finishes to the perfect flow of the bracelet and individual links into the case.

From a purely mechanical standpoint, the B/1 is a well-made and well-finished piece of horology. Underneath the unusual case shape—which, as photos reveal, is not flat—beats a Swiss-made Sellita SW100 calibre ticking at 28,800 BPH (4Hz) with a 38-hour power reserve. Beneath a flat sapphire crystal lies a jaw-dropping lapis lazuli dial, complemented by a set of Dauphine-style hands with the hour hand's tip brutally slashed off. The case and bracelet as a whole display an intricate alternation of brushed and micro-blasted finishes (almost concrete-looking), which gently reflect the light in intriguing ways. And all this can be yours for $4,000, a reasonable price considering the design and attention to detail. (A feat made possible as the B/1 is made, assembled, and quality-controlled in China, a fact that should objectively not matter one bit.)

And by this very fact, the B/1 constitutes somewhat of a middle finger pointed at the luxury Swiss watch industry, which often matches its horological creations with exorbitant price tags. As if art and beauty should be reserved for a chosen few. The privilege of being an artist, says Toledano, is to make something new that you like, not something that should please others or be endowed with specific seals of approval. The Toledano & Chan B/1 proves that original, quality horology can be within reach of a larger swath of the watch collector community. And that excellence doesn't have to be outrageously expensive.

toledano&chan

BEYOND DEATH THESE LIVE

BEYOND TIME FLESH DEATH

Photographer & Stylist
Motoki Nakatani
@motokinakatani

Models
Alice Zonca
@zoncalice
Marine Zonca
@marinezonca
Quentin

Watches
@arthuroduro
@ontherocks

Omega De Ville

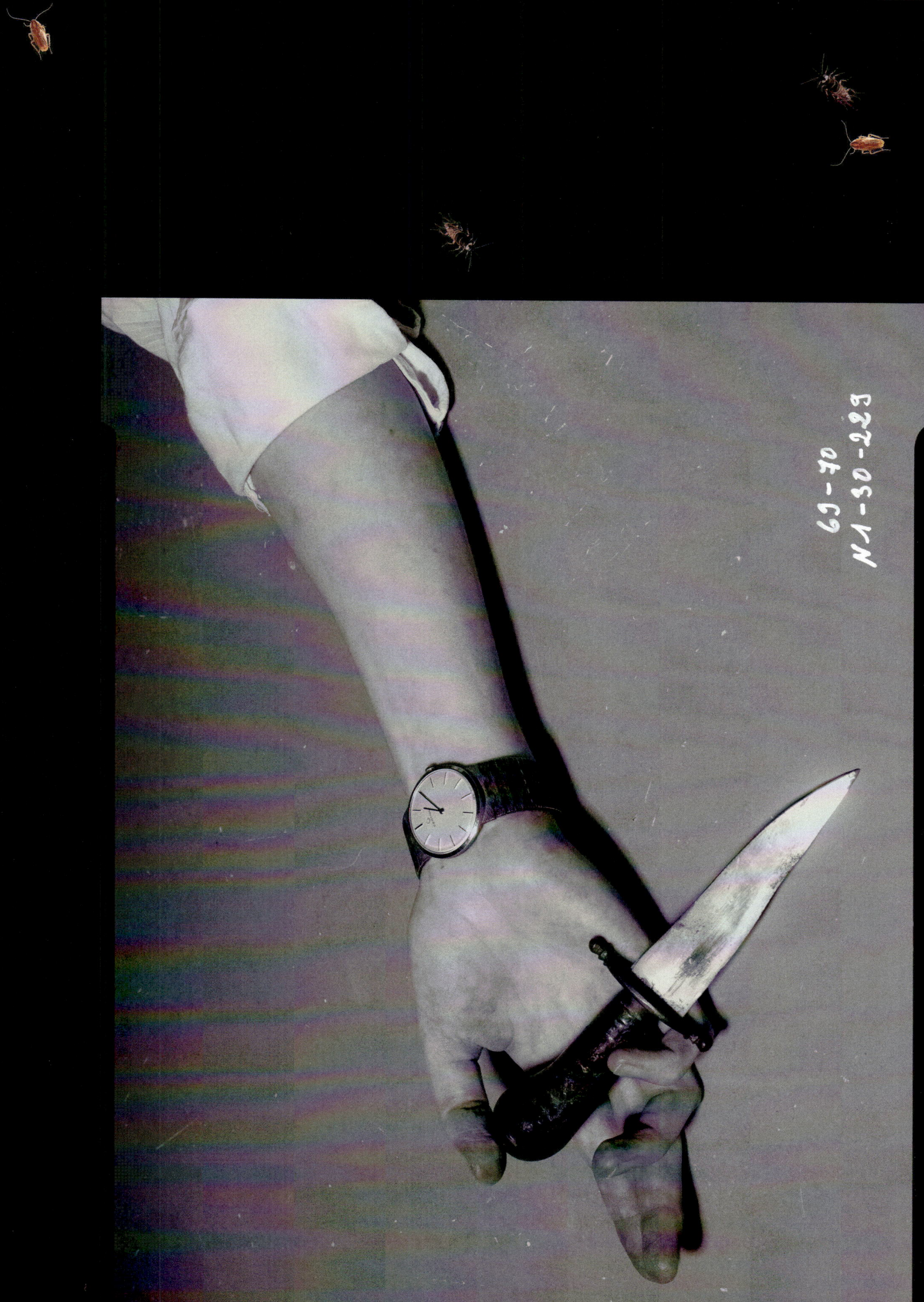
69-70
N1-30-229

Rolex Bubble Back

Patek Philippe ref. 2526

M-662 597
1-30 -22

305812
337-20-5

Graphic Designer: Jeffrey Thomson and Scarlett Baker

GIRL TALK

Words by Scarlett Baker

The canon of women's watches has long been chastised as "petite" and "demure," as recent as 2023 (*Vogue*). But if we're going to talk about what women want, why not start by actually asking them? Isn't it high time we talked about what the female gaze actually entails, in a bid to finally fathom just what makes women tick?

I'm sitting in a populated square in the centre of Geneva's old town. The din of convivial chatter permeates as much as the plumes of breathy smoke from cigarettes. Revellers congregate for an apéro with friends, and adjacent to my table, a woman lifts an acidulous-looking cornichon from her plate to her lips. As she does so, her sleeve peels away from her arm, revealing the corners of a watch. In this sudden moment of espionage, I'm determined to deduce its identity, and for the duration that it takes to consume a glass of wine, a Gerald Genta Mickey Mouse from 2021 is finally discerned. Excellent choice. A new entourage has just joined the social circus of the dining square, consisting of three women, two bearing watches, while the other a lonely wrist. I spy a CASIO and an Omega Constellation with a gem-set bezel that looks like it's lived a good life. Amid this nucleus of merrymakers, no two watches fastened to the wrists of female wearers are the same. This small congregation alone is enough to reveal that a woman's watch follows no formula.

"Fashion reveals itself as the most reliable cultural mirror we own," penned author Norbert Stern in Mode und Kultur (1914), and I would agree. To an extent. 'What do you want to say to the world today?' is embedded into the clothes we don, just as much as the stitches that hold them together. As a result, this second skin that we are personally entangled with, both physically in the act of covering our bodies and emotionally, allows us to discover someone's inner workings, and at large, learn about the greater mood of the zeitgeist. But a watch is something more than that, which is why I'd politely modify Stern's

THROUGH THE LOOKING GLASS

statement, replacing 'fashion' with 'the watch' instead.

The watch reveals itself as the most reliable cultural mirror we own, not because it's a unit of measure to govern time and thus encourage us to be prompt and reliable beings, but because it distinguishes the difference between material objects as necessity and of desire. Hear me out: the act of dressing ourselves in clothes, stylish or otherwise, is to fundamentally cover our bodies, while a watch is merely an addition. I don't have to tell you twice that there's no need to wear a watch, but if we're to view watches as a mirror of society, surely it's a superlative method of discovering exactly what the heart wants – or loathes.

So what does this looking glass reveal about women and their relationship with telling the time?

ONCE UPON A TIME

What the mirror reveals in its reflection right now is that there are slight cracks that need bonding with something more robust than a little bit of tape. The untapped potential of the female consumer is crucial, and the bond between brand and consumer is paramount, with two-thirds of women buying watches for their own use, according to Deloitte's Swiss Watch Industry 2023. But corporate jargon aside, what the fuck do women want from their watch? "A great watch is a soul with a story," offers New York-based watch zealot Jessica Vega. "If my watch is set and working properly, I feel held." A great watch communicates well, and we're not talking timekeeping accuracy here - it comes major down to the story behind it. Take the canon of women's watch advertisements for instance. If you've never gone down this rabbit hole, I urge you to get comfy with the archive on your next rainy day and feast on the farcical relics of bygone eras. "Almost as complicated as a woman. Except it's on time," penned IWC in the early 2000s. You have to laugh (and elicit audible gasps). If not for the gumption, then for the realisation that it's *so* dated, even the contact address on the ad boasts an @aol.com handle. Old news.

While I'm not about to shit on all my fellow women here, the ad *is* punchy for its frivolity, and it's one of many in IWC's historic slogans to bring satire to the watch, something that feels distant today in how watchmaking is visually communicated. It's one of the few advertisements that have stained my memory (casual sexism aside), for its ability to place the watch in a narrative beyond function. We talk about these timepieces being our companions, and yet when we market them, we strip them of their voice and focus on the science of their existence, rather than what it actually means to be conceived. Now, I'm not saying "Let's do a 180 and plaster 'Behind Every Great Man is a Great Woman." in the next ad campaign, but let's spare a thought for more prudent storytelling, shall we?

Watch enthusiast, Victoria Cattin, is mutually frowning. "Storytelling of most watch brands is not great enough. There's a lot to learn on this end, and brands could definitely take a page from the book of fashion to create a more immersive experience."

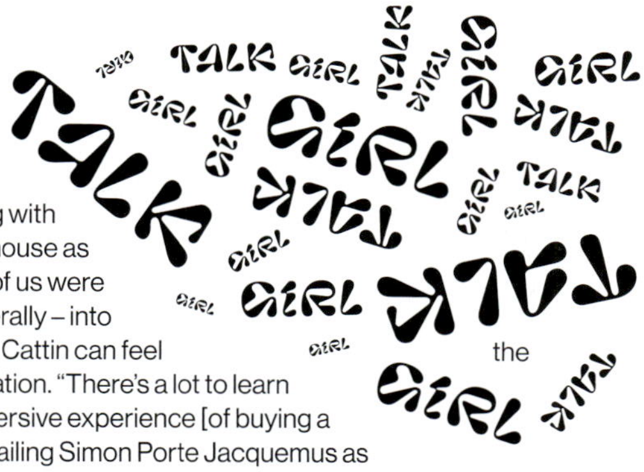

Born into a lineage of watchmakers, playing with watches around the house as a child while the rest of us were sinking our teeth – literally – into dolls and plastic toys, Cattin can feel the abscence of narration. "There's a lot to learn to create a more immersive experience [of buying a watch]" she shares, hailing Simon Porte Jacquemus as the blueprint.

Jacquemus' name rears its head a few times amongst this round table of women looking in on what watches are, and what they are not. Watchmaker and CEO of Charriol, an established Swiss watchmaker and jeweller, Coralie Charriol, was walking through the fetching streets of Paris, noticing a man across from her, dressed in smart attire with Jacquemus' viral Le Petit Chiquito across his shoulders, a bag so small that a solo bank card might just fit. From hosting collections typically outside of

fashion weeks, to running a provocative Instagram account, his penchant for playfulness permeates the Jacquemus lens bridging the union between consumer and brand closer together, as opposed to a more stilted corporate approach.
While the watch world has a lot to learn from the fashion industry, it treads a fine line too. 'Fashion watches,' for the

STOP WITH THE SLURS

horologically uninitiated, reads like a curse word. Consider it a slur to the superlative watches that are mechanically Swiss Made (typically considered the creme de la creme of watchmaking, given the country's dexterous relationship with watchmaking). Living in a society that favours categorisations and rationality, a watch made by a fashion house struggles to become something other than a fashion watch, while a fashionable-looking watch created by a watch brand remains as that. And for the most part, the former is aimed at women following the crescendo of fashion watches in the aftermath of the 1970s quartz crisis.
While it might seem rational from the industry's gatekeepers to call fashion watches as such, there's actually something highly irrational about it. Fashion watches are, more often than not, the by-product of a major label with an emphasis on design first and movement second. But how can you put something so revolutionary as a ceramic Chanel J12 in the same fodder as a Michael Kors? The answer: You just can't. Fundamentally, "a fashion watch is a watch created through a licensee with a low price point," shares Charriol. "People tried to put us there because we made watches with cable bracelets and it was different. It was fashionable, but that doesn't make it a fashion watch." Shedding the label, Charriol has championed an approach to women's watchmaking since the 1980s, under the helm of her watchmaker father, Philippe Charriol. Carrying the legacy of her father's brand that prioritised women's watches with a design edge, Charriol's work exposes the liminal space in women's watches that dabbles between a watch and a piece of jewellery. "As a female watchmaker, the challenge is to be considered and included amongst other watch brands, in order to solidify my legitimacy," she continues. "When you mainly work on ladies watches, you often fall out of the club of watchmaking and they put you under the label of creating fashion-led watches."
Google will tell you we're currently at the apex of jewellery-inspired watches, (ie. watches befitted with gems, gold bracelets That transition from the wrist to the neck, finger,

"Alarm watches, water-resistant watches, stop-watches, watches for day wear, for sport, for evening...Watches for every manner of man. And what watches the Swiss make for women! Gold watches, watches set among diamonds, watches on bangles, ring-watches, brooch-watches [...] Look at that girl's face" (1955).

"Circle her wrist with diamonds," cried Bulova two decades later. Ushering both creative and destructive powers, the maelstrom of conversation when it comes to diamonds is that they belong on a woman's wrist. And while this isn't a vendetta against Marilyn Monroe's famous sentiment, the diamond debate is tired, and frankly if Lucy wants to be in the sky with diamonds, then it's entirely Lucy's choice. There's no one answer for whether women want diamonds on their watch, because there's no one woman.
Befittingly, in the time it takes for Rihanna to sing the chorus of 'Diamonds,' I've discovered ten watch brands promoting diamond watches as the first product on the women's section page. We can oscillate between love and hate, critique and praise all day, but the fact is, women's watches hierarchisye these gem-studded models as the premier choice.
If this microcosmic jury of voices you find in these pages is anything to go by, it's that there isn't a single answer, and thus, it's high time we stopped viewing the design choices as something pejorative, but instead as, a preference. It's the same tirade against Mother of Pearl, too. Some of us like it, some of us don't.

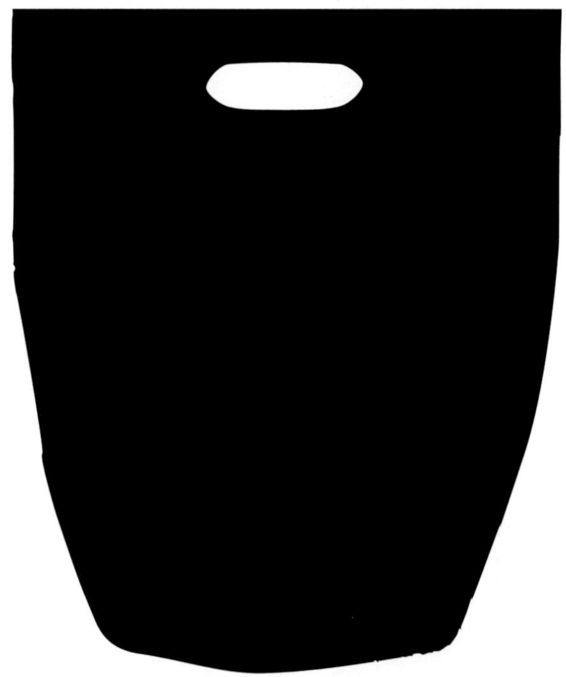

or even belt loop, thanks to Cartier's latest carabiner-clock offering). But frankly, as women, we're rejecting the notion that this is just a trend. Allow me to unpack.

Noun /trend/ – a general direction in which something is developing or changing.

A trend is something in flux, a transitory state from one thing to another, and to define this current of design-focused watches, that have long been created for women's wrists, eliminates women's sartorial tastes as something less than permanent in the catalogue. "I absolutely believe that watches are pretty much jewellery," notes jeweller Nadine Ghosn, whose whimsical creations from Crayola-inspired cuffs to stackable burger rings are as valuable to her as her love for watches. "If you look at people's wristwatches, half the time they aren't on time, which goes to show it's more of an accessory and statement in today's style, than a functionality." For sure, we're certainly seeing a resurgence in the hedonism of the 70's aesthetic which places a spotlight on eclecticism and extravagance (looking at you Piaget Polo 79). Further to that, the litany of stone dials that dominated throughout the swinging 60s are back in vogue, a popular aesthete during the quartz crisis when cheaper watches witnessed a chokehold. Even though we're witnessing a symbiosis of accessory and utility, dubbed by The New York Times as the trend of 2024, us gals would merely argue that its us merely entering the group

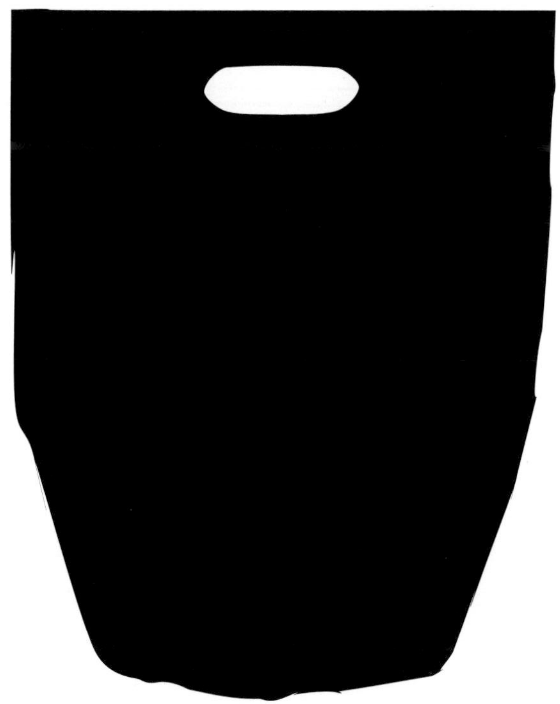

chat for good and the watches that we favour that spotlight aesthetic, are finally getting the recognition our wrists deserve. "My favourite watch designs speak to me just as loudly as my favourite jewellery," agrees luxury consultant, Jodie Marie Smith. "Watches and jewellery can function completely differently, or almost identically. Both jewellery and watches communicate whatever the wearer desires, and can be deeply personal expressions or entirely strategic displays of wealth or design knowledge - and can even be both at once." Case in point, Andrew Grima's 'Greenland' watch, 1970, from the 'About Time' collection for Omega is my ultimate grail. To me, the yellow gold with pink tourmaline 'glass' in an exploding shape is the perfect combination of watch and jewellery design."

THE STONE AGE

But here's where it gets tricky when we start talking about jewellery-inspired watches for women. And best believe we're hailing back to those thorny watch adverts from yesteryear.

Embracing her male partner, and thanking him for the gift of her diamond cocktail watch, the Swiss Federation of Watch Manufacturers pens:

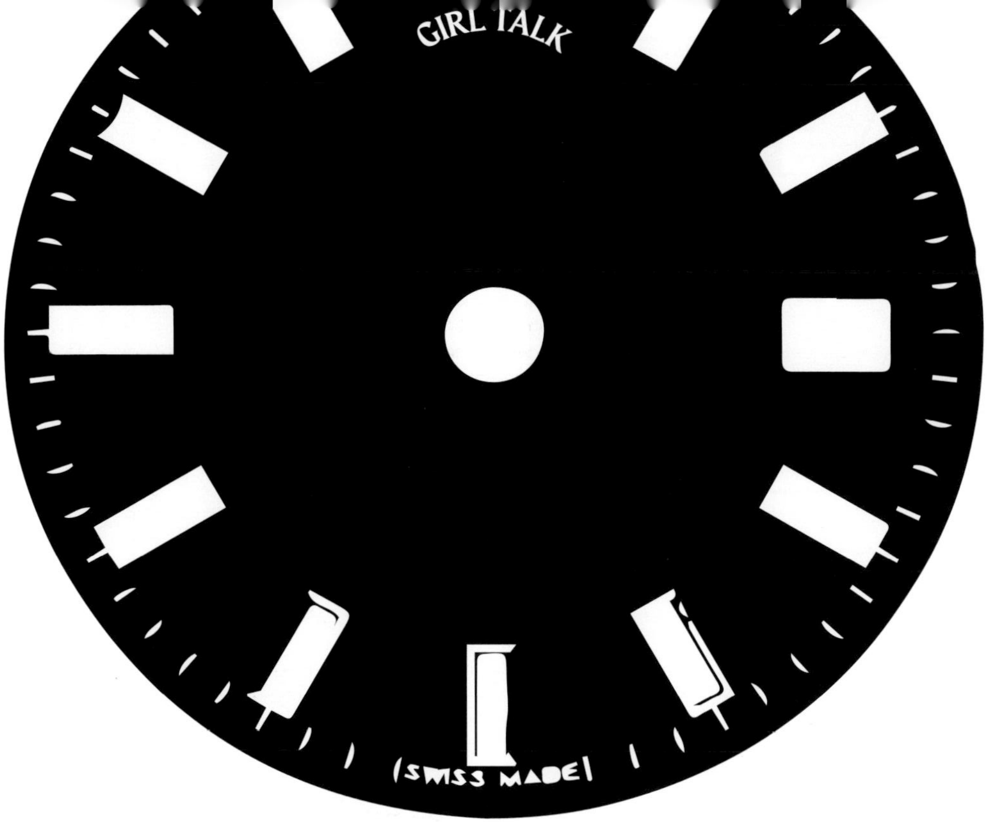

Graphic Designer: Jeffrey Thomson and Scarlett Baker

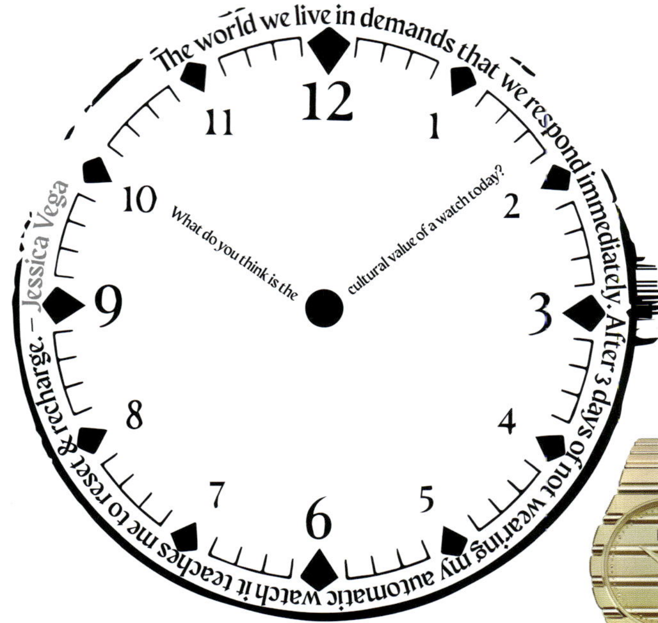

Piaget Polo 79

Bulgari Monete Montre

Do you give a fuck about diamonds on a watch?

Not really! Most of my watches do not have diamonds on them. VC

Not my thing. Perhaps glam, but out of reach. MC

If it's factory and done tastefull, I'm here for it. Talking to you 5196P. JV

A woman's watch needs to have diamonds. It's like, I don't know, it's part of it. It's like the fantasy of a watch, if you will. CC

I value simplicity or audacity. One or the other, small diamonds around the face are not my thing. either it is seriously simple or fully paved. NG

Bulgari Serpenti Secret

'This diamond, flawless
My diamond, flawless
This rock, flawless
My rock, flawless'

Flawless, Beyoncé (2013)

When Blancpain conceived the Ladybird Colours Collection, or Van Cleef & Arpels their Perlée 23mm watch in 18-karat rose gold with mother of pearl, they didn't do so to fuel the sparring of #TeamPearl or otherwise. Call it a cliché, or call it one of the toughest materials on the planet. The point is, we women don't care to sit here and shit talk Mother of Pearl. After all, its namesake comes from the belief that the mother nacre mollusc shields and protects the pearl, in the same way a mother cuddles her child. "It brings us a little bit of our day-to-day," reflects Charriol, who riffs on using the material throughout her work. "It's age old and it brings a beautiful iridescence. C'est vivant. More than anything, it's about innovation and the possibilities of what you can do with a watch."

That said, we don't need to be perpetually bulldozed about all things bussed down or pearly, just because this vision once favoured daintier wrists. Women don't *just* want diamonds or pink-tinged dials, but it's OK to want them, too. Back in the yesteryear of 2006, *Europa Star*, one of the oldest watch magazines in existence, coined that "in women's watches, watches with diamonds sell faster and better than the same watches without diamonds." Today, the attitude has shifted, with diamonds a woman's frontier because they are the self-purchasers making the vote for themselves. It's the oversaturation of marketing techniques that drives the debate into a for and against mentality, when in fact, all of us women want is to feel confident in our choice because it's ours and it speaks to our personality. This divisive misconception around what a woman wants echoes right through to the store fronts that we window shop in, too. "It can be a very alienating feeling," reflects Mojdeh Cutter, Head of Partnerships at the Swiss Institute and Managing Director of the biennial auction, TimeForArt. "It's similar to going into a high-level commercial art gallery and feeling judged and out of place," indicative of

Hermès Nantucket Sertie Neige

Bulgari Serpenti Spiga Montre

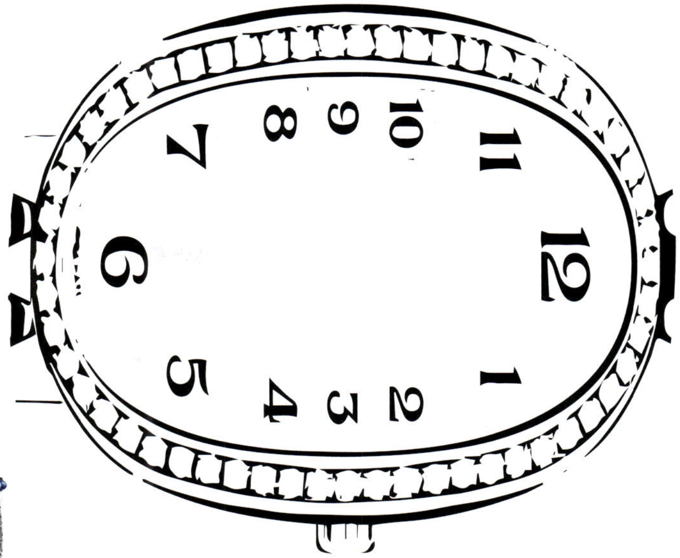

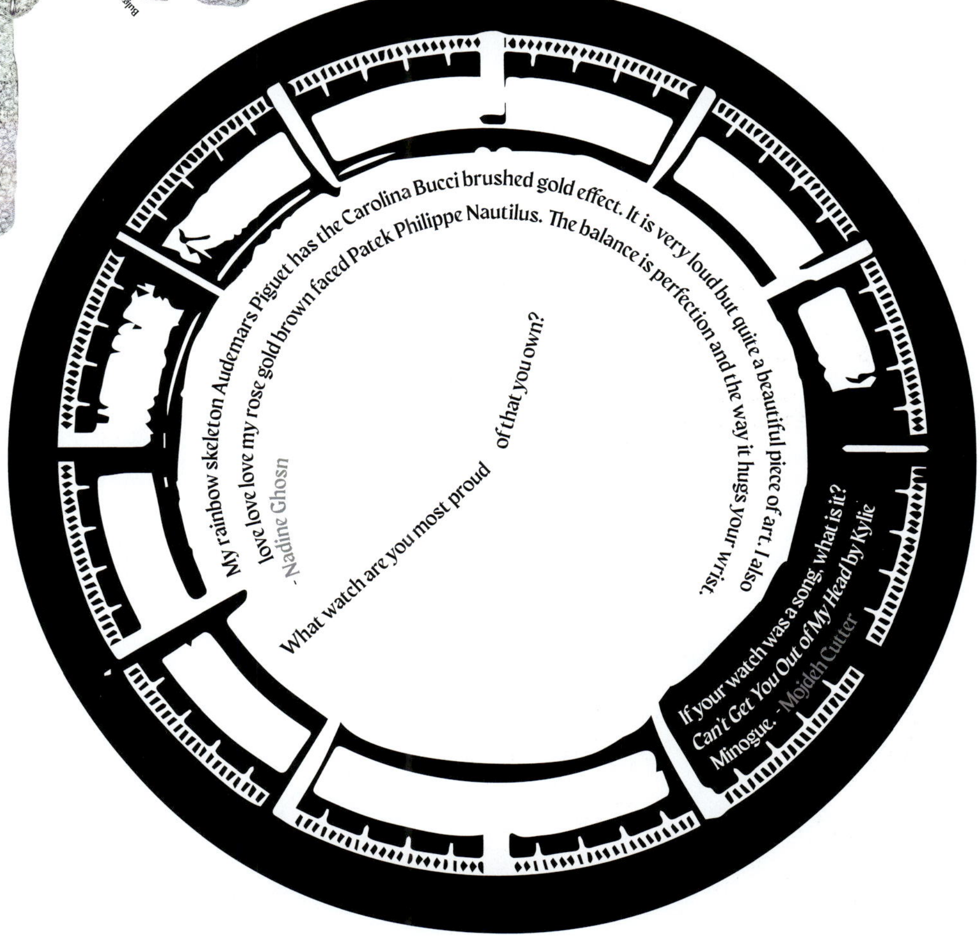

when women are often ushered towards the freshly polished glass booths in stores, titled 'Ladies Watches' with gemstones in their plenty glaring up at you. "I usually end up leaving wishing I had unlimited resources and could prove the store employees wrong."

THE MIRRORED DIAL

It all comes back to the allegorical mirror and the fear that brands only allow their customer to see what they think they ought to be seeing, prioritising the needs of a woman from the past. The retail mirror is a thwarted one at best, allowing bodies to scrutinise and compare themselves. "Each day, I witnessed people study, scrutinise, and compare their bodies before the wall-sized mirror. No matter how favourable their assessment, the fitting rooms were fraught with the relics of a lifetime of insidious, internalised notions of what a body – especially, a woman's body – should look like," pens researcher and art historian, Sarah Bochicchio. We ought to be wary of perpetuating a ruthless reflection that suggests it's wrong to like diamonds, but wrong to not. Weird to like flowers, but not weird if not. If we continue to give noise to the debate, we'll only eviscerate the potential of both.

If the mirror of a woman's reflection reveals anything, it's that we as humans are shape-shifting beings, decreed by change. Women's watches are a moving target, just as much as men's, that deserve to evolve. After all, these little ticking canvases that we bestow on our bodies are a locus of public display but with private intent. The relationship between the watch and its wearer differs from person to person. Still, through this unique experience with our greatest luxury of all, every voice should be seen through the reflective powers of a watch, beyond just the sapphire that glares back at you.

Graphic Designer: Jeffrey Thomson and Scarlett Baker

Hermès Kelly

JODIE MARIE SMITH, LUXURY CONSULTANT

@jodiemariesmith

Do you wear a watch? If so, why, and if not, why not?
Day-to-day I wear my husband's Casio F-91W, which I liked initially out of aggressive practicality and my tendency to wear a lot of black. Then, I read @ watchesofespionage's post on it which totally sold me on wearing one of the most ubiquitous watches in the world, which has such a fascinating cultural significance.

How far do you see the role of the watch today as an accessory?
The watch is often seen too strictly as a STATUS SYMBOL rather than an extension of one's personal taste or style. I'm hopeful that this is starting to change and people are starting to feel like being more experimental and diverse in their watch wearing and collecting.

Are there any that you've found that you'd add to your wish list?
My watch wishlist features variations of 70s vintage Piaget models in textured white gold with opal or decorative hard stone dials, Patcharavipa's reworked 80s Audemars Piguet's, and most of Pierre Cardin's timepieces.

Describe your dream watch.
Andrew Grima's 'Greenland' watch, 1970, from the 'About Time' collection by Andrew Grima for Omega. To me, the yellow gold with pink tourmaline 'glass' in an exploding shape dial is the perfect combination of watch and jewellery design.

The watch isn't something that just belongs on the wrist. Are you open to wearing it elsewhere on the body, ie. choker, ring?
I bought AVAVAV's triple watch face 'FAUX-LEX' choker a year ago, but now we're really in the apex of that trend. I love that the design purposely celebrates the modern icon that is the fake Rolex, in this obvious, ostentatious way. Even though it's costume jewellery, the three watches still have personal resonance - as a British transplant in San Francisco, I have each watch set to different time zones for the friends, family and clients on the West and East coasts of the US, and at home.

VICTORIA CATTIN, MARKETING SPECIALIST

@victoriacattin

What's your earliest memory of wearing a watch?
I actually come from a family of French watchmakers (3 generations before me), so I always grew up around watches. Even though my dad left the industry when I was younger and rejoined recently, I always had tons of watches in my house and played around with them as a kid.

How often do you wear a watch now? Can you talk us through your collection? How do you feel when you wear a watch?
Almost every single day since I know how to read time. I usually feel NAKED without my jewellery and a

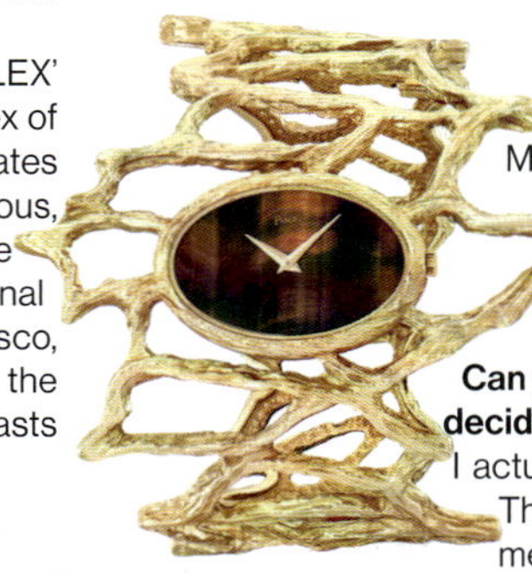
Piaget Archive Cuff (1978)

MOJDEH CUTTER, HEAD OF PARTNERSHIPS, SWISS INSTITUTE

@notmyrodeo

Can you remember the first watch you had fastened to your wrist? What was it like?
I don't remember which came first - my Baby-G or my Flik-Flak. Both are so iconic – I occasionally think about wearing them again to indulge in nostalgia.

What do you yearn for in the world of watches?

More women CEOs!

What's your guilty pleasure of a watch?
The Gucci 1900L series. Painfully 2000s and perfect.

What prompted you to buy your first watch? Can you talk us through the process and how you decided?
I actually haven't ever bought myself a watch... yet. The watches I own were very generously gifted to me and passed down by my parents. I would love to buy myself a watch but having to decide which one will be my first purchase is paralyzing.

How do you feel about design-based watches and this dominant resurgence for the likes of Cartier and Piaget?
Absolutely love it. I am a Cartier girl through and through (learned from my mother). Coming from the art world, design has always been my first access point into watches.

How do you feel about flowers on the dial? Are there any brands that you feel have mastered this without leaning into the stereotype of womens watches? 🌼🌼🌼🌼🌼🌼🌼🌼
Never been a fan of flower motifs – pass!

What do you think is the cultural value of a watch today?
Self-expression.

Who are your style icons?
"Love. Angel. Music. Baby." era from Gwen Stefani.

Do you give a fuck about diamonds on a watch?
No :) 💎💎💎💎💎💎💎💎💎

Would a watch be more appealing to you if you knew the involvement of the women who created it?
Definitely. Especially when you knew the artisans behind each métiers d'art.

Pair a watch of your choosing with each mood: Mellow, Spontaneous, Giggly
Mellow: Cartier Tank Francaise
Spontaneous: M.A.D. 1 by MB&F
Giggly: Hello Kitty Flik Flak

Hermès Kelly

JESSICA VEGA,
WATCH DEALER

@stillnessvega

What's your earliest memory of wearing a watch? Can you recall what it?
I'm thinking it was the Rugrats Reptar watch with a hologram dial exclusive to Burger King in '98. Seven-year-old me tried to become a collector because I really attempted to buy the whole set.
What prompted you to buy your first watch?
Synchronicity, I haven't ever set out in search of a new watch, but if a new watch opportunity presents itself I usually listen to my gut and haven't had any regrets

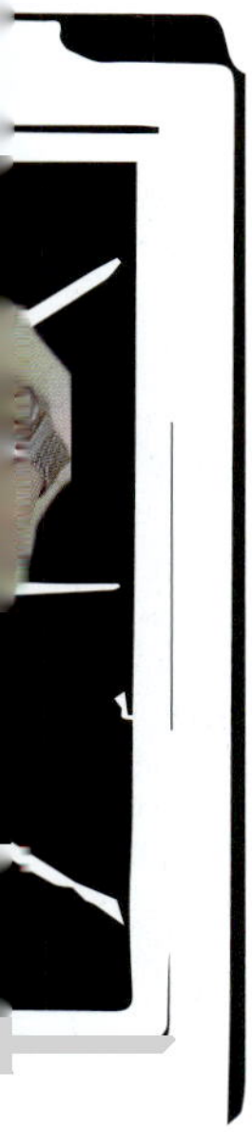

watch. I own too many vintage watches from the 60s/70s from small brands, but I wear my Cartier panther the most since I got it last December. I also have a steel OMEGA Seamaster 38 with diamond index, a small Longines, a blue Hublot classic fusion. Each piece has a sentimental value, I don't think that I could sell any of them.
How far do you think objects can be beautiful, and not just created for a moment in time?
I don't think that there is a limit, particularly when talking about the watch industry. I went to the Patek Philippe Museum during my last visit to Geneva in December and I would have worn every watch that they had if I could have.
Would a watch be more appealing to you if you knew the involvement of the women who created it?
Perhaps. I have recently developed a fascination with JLC, and the fact that Catherine Rénier is their CEO only adds to my admiration for them.
Pair a watch of your choosing with each mood: Angry, Curious, Chaotic.
Angry: The Moonswatches. For some reason this collaboration makes me angry.
Curious: The Jaeger-LeCoultre Reverso
Chaotic: Definitely the RM 69.

When you think of time, what does it make you think of?
Community, accessibility and privilege.
What do you think is the cultural value of a watch today?
The world we live in demands that we respond immediately. After three days of not wearing my automatic watch it teaches me to reset and recharge.
Would a watch be more appealing to you if you knew the involvement of the women who created it?

A watch designed by authentic inspiration is appealing to me.
If your watch was a song, what would it be?
Apple Tree by Erykah Badu.

NADINE GHOSN,
JEWELLERY DESIGNER

@nadineghosnjewelery

Audemars Piguet Royal Oak Frosted Gold Double Balance Wheel Openworked

"Rainbow"

Can you remember your first watch?
As a kid my first watches were the plastic watches with a maze inside I used to get them from my dentist. My first functioning watch was a G-Shock. I was obsessed with the fact that it glowed in the dark.
How do you feel about diamonds on a watch? Do they speak to you?
I value simplicity or audacity. One or the other, small DIAMONDS around the face are not my thing. Either it is seriously simple or fully PAVED.
What do you think the secret ingredient is to bringing more women into the world of watches, even if just purchasing their first one?
Speaking about them, wearing and pairing them. I find that many of my clients start to appreciate or like a watch once they see it worn by people whose style inspires them.
Is there an iconic styling moment or women wearing a watch that is ingrained in your memory?
I always love to wear two watches. I am trying to think of someone wearing a watch that inspired me, I would say probably Victoria Beckham and Jennifer Aniston like 15 years ago they would wear the Rolex President in full gold as like a cool wrist bracelet.

CORALIE CHARRIOL,
WATCHMAKER + CEO

@coraliecharriol

Where lies the ultimate challenge for women and watches?
As a female watchmaker, it's being considered and included amongst the others in order to solidify my legitimacy. When you mainly work on ladies watches, you often fall out of the club of watchmaking and they put you under the label of creating fashion watches.
consumer, is purchasing it, right?
Where do you think we're missing the mark in addressing women?
I am a female watchmaker. I am also the daughter of a watchmaker, and I've learned it's about how you communicate the details. It's about storytelling. You talk to a woman who's purchasing her first watch and you say GMT, how are you supposed to know what that is? But tell her that her kids are in New York and she's in LA and she needs a watch with Dual Time Zones. It's about educating in a way that never feels patronising and adapted to a woman's life. It should be women telling it to women.

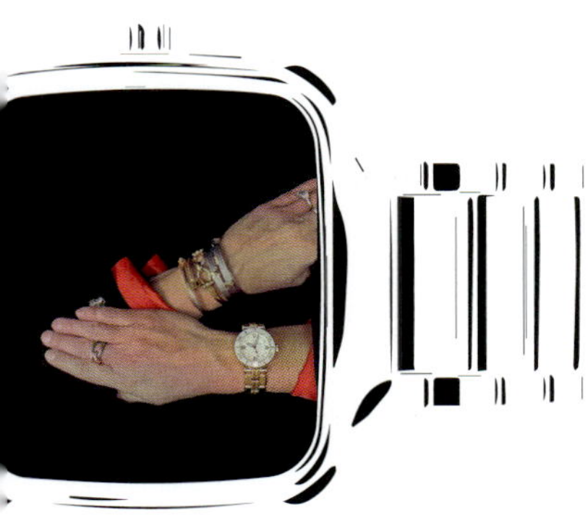

Words from the Intern

Words from the Intern

I stole a few pages so the youth

Hey there, I'm Rémi, the intern hired by Maxime and Lorenzo. In a nutshell, I'm the guy who brews the coffee and handles the shitty chores. I've managed to hijack four pages of this mag to share something cool with you. To cut a long story short, I'm fed up with their constant nattering about ancient timepieces with eye-watering price tags. Audemars Piguet this, Rolex that. Sure, these are fine pieces of craftsmanship. But on the pittance they toss me, I'd be able to afford one in half a century. Let's face it: these are old-timer brands. And I'd also like to prove that penning articles about these watches isn't as complicated as they make it out to be. Fair warning: if you're a watch enthusiast north of 30, you might want to skip what comes next. Because I'm about to tell you about a watch that's worlds apart from your precious "Swiss Made." The watch I'm about to unfold comes from a brand you're undoubtedly clued up on—the notorious American streetwear titan, Nike. Yep, Nike didn't just create clothing and trainers. Back in the early 2000s, Nike was busy collaborating with indie designers to whip up more than just apparel: backpacks, caps, and other spin-off merch. But we're here to discover their wristwear. To achieve their ends, Nike would often whisk their designers away on "creative trips" to spark a blaze of product ideas. One of them, Phil Frank, an American, lucked out on these trips. He was flung into the TV show 'Junkyard Wars', where the goal was to cobble together solutions to challenges from scraps found in a scrapyard.

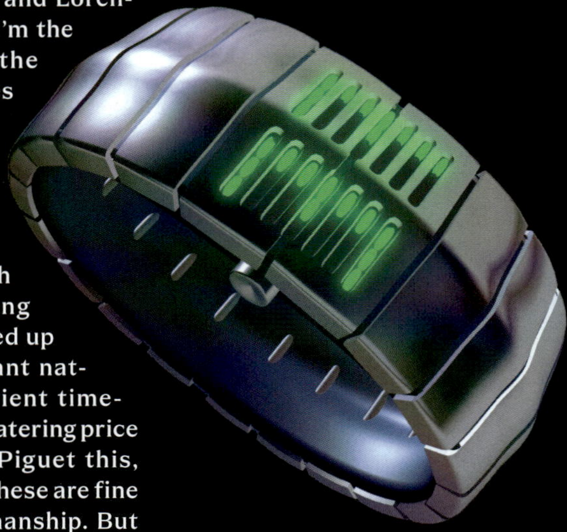

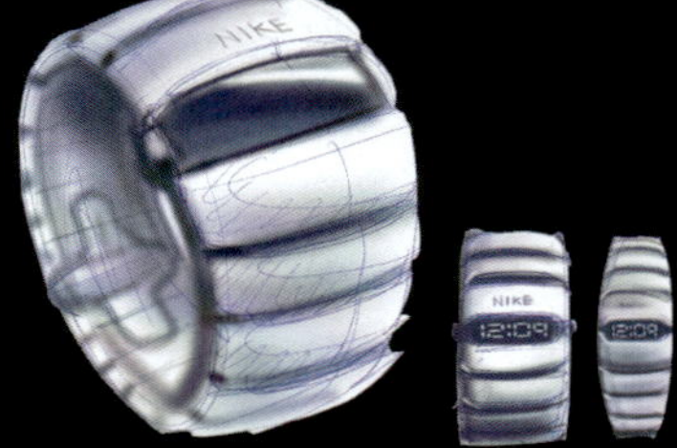

has a voice in this maga-zine

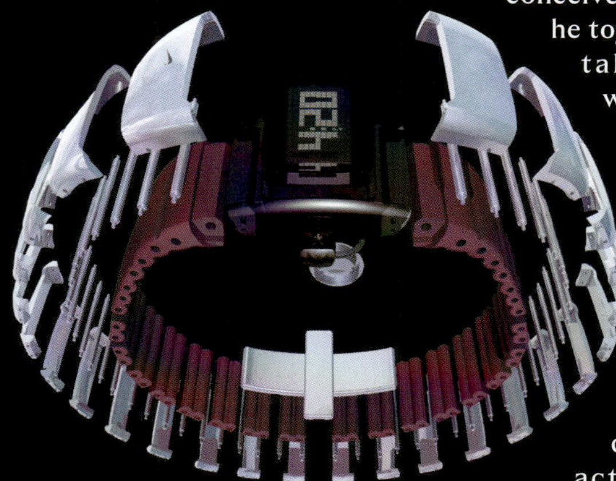

You guessed it—Phil's crew clinched the win. It'd be too long to narrate the whole experience, but the gist is that Phil drew heaps of inspiration from this contest and was already busy sketching up his future masterpiece. Before Phil conceived the final product, he toyed with the 'Crystaless' concept—a watch with a futuristic blueprint. His idea was to pair an inner silicone strip with outer metal links (think tank treads), some pulling double duty with openings acting as LED windows, showing time in an innovative format. One window would display scrolling digits, while the other mimicked an equaliser, with bars marking hours and minutes. It's time to roll out the iconic Nike Watch D-Line Collection and spill why I've nicked these four pages. Following the 'Crystaless' trail, the silicone band and metal links stuck. But reading time got a facelift—out with the small futuristic windows, in with a display. The watch took on a more down-to-earth look while keeping its swanky design. Aside from being a nice-looking watch, the D-Line boasts a few interesting features. And no, I'm not waffling on about a perpetual calendar or some other daft complication that watch buffs slobber over. We're talking USEFUL stuff here. An alarm, a stopwatch, and water resistance up to 7 bars. Handy features for all those divers out there! Nike hit the jackpot with the D-Line, flying off shelves worldwide and laying the groundwork for numerous collabs. This watch bridged generations with its pioneering design. That's it for the D-Line. If you've had a good read, fire an email to info@apresdemain.watch and haggle for a raise for the poor intern forced to steal the pages of a magazine to make a splash.

Dare to Dream

The grand Geneva week has just wrapped up, and we're faced with the usual post-event question, "So, seen anything stunning?" I'm at a loss for words! I've certainly seen things, and yes, some were strikingly beautiful, but they're in the minority! Let's set the record straight: I'm not part of the growing minority that pines for the 'good old days' of vintage horology. I'm of the view that my children would prefer to inherit watches imbued with my own stories rather than those from strangers of the 1930s, even if they come with Gay Frères bracelets, Hagmann cases, and Stern dials of the era. Judging by the overheard squabbles among my kids, it seems I'm right. They've already divided up my watches posthumously! This impatient youth! Fear not; I plan to keep them waiting a bit longer, thank you very much! So, not being a fanatic of yesteryear's fine watchmaking, I firmly believe that today's horology is brimming with tantalising promises—it's high time it delivered on them! Like a child awaits Christmas, I've been starry-eyed for the annual salon weeks for twenty years, only to find that stars can quickly turn into black holes, much to my regret.You might argue that I'm hard to please, that the 500-plus new releases at Watches and Wonders should be enough, or at least I could cling to some residual stardust. But come on, brand friends, make us dream: cease with the mere colour, size, and material changes. True creation begins when the gimmicks end! Of course, criticism is easy from where I stand, not having to satisfy those Excel spreadsheet bottom lines. And yet... Yet, some watchmakers toil and break records of slimness, with a 2mm tourbillon, or a COSC-certified watch at 1.7mm; this may not fuel my dreams, but I can understand it igniting others'. Yet, the quest for precision, which, let's remember, is no longer of any practical use in the jewellery that watches have become, continues to drive the lofty calculations of horologists: a moon phase deviating by one day every 45 million years, does that not launch you on a quest among the stars with your intergalactic vessel? It does for me. Yet, some designers truly sketch with the Great Old Ones in mind (and I'm not referring to Lovecraft's). Parmigiani Fleurier's creation of the ultimate sartorial watch is a perfect example. When one knows the design of the original Toric, one can only applaud the masterful way in which the challenge has been met and conquered. Yet, some brands take the artisanship out of its soppy comfort zone; Czapek's gravitational wave enamel is simply mesmerising! You get it, brand friends. The wellspring of creativity is not dead. It's buried, indeed, and it demands hard work, undeniably, but it's very much alive. So, don't hesitate to step out of the box—you might just be surprised by what you uncover. As for me, I'll always be grateful to Pandora for closing her box; the hope of being surprised endures.

En route to Paris—18.04.2024—Soundtrack: "Incendie" by Noir Désir—LGM

In many respects, watch brands seem keen on enlightening the youth. If executive interviews are anything to go by, this fresh-faced generation is the new El Dorado. It's the must-win crowd set to rescue the industry from the looming Asian disinterest. Like good troopers, the communication departments of our hero brands have thus rallied to the cause. And since the youth are allegedly uninitiated, these departments have, for some years, taken to schooling them with jargon via press releases and websites. Here's a quick review of words and their definitions (lifted from the Dictionary), without which a press release heralding THE latest thing wouldn't quite cut it. **Versatile** — in French, it denotes someone fickle or prone to sudden changes of heart. It's a 'false friend' of the English versatile, meaning "able to adapt or be adapted to many different functions or activities" (Cambridge Dictionary). The most accurate translation in French would be 'polyvalent', which, granted, lacks a bit of panache! **Quintessence** — the most perfect or typical example of a quality or class. **Pinnacle** — In its most literal sense, it refers to the highest point, like the crowning point of the Temple of Jerusalem. In Gothic architecture, it's the slender, pyramid-like structure that caps the abutments and flying buttresses. Figuratively speaking, when someone is "placed on a pinnacle," they're held in the highest esteem by others. **Ultimate** — Coming last in a series or process.

Let's cap this list here. I'm not entirely sure the brands' communicators grasped the true meaning of these terms! Sure, the intent to expand the youth's (and everyone else's) vocabulary is commendable, but within our domain, at worst, it's insulting and, at best, pretentious. I'm not sure which I prefer. We'll also gloss over the avalanche of superlatives and adjectives that proliferate brand communication to the point of nausea. The purpose of product communication is to tell its story—plain and simple. There's no need to dress it up with convoluted vocabulary (triple word score) when this story is written by the many hands that imagine, design, create, embellish, and sell this timepiece. How many passionate workers have developed wondrous systems without mention of their dogged determination? How many finishers, polishers, inspectors, adjusters, decorators, pad printers, electroplaters, and turners have toiled to breathe life into these marvels from another age? Shouldn't we just tell the real stories sans superlatives and glitter? The younger crowd thirsts for authenticity. They're curious, unencumbered by pretence, and not easily fooled. The grand, luxuriously historic displays often fall on deaf ears among them. If the brands were brave enough to engage, they might find themselves pleasantly surprised. The youth crave the genuine and authentic, not the hollow proclamations from out-of-touch urban agencies, whose vacuous words mirror only their profound ignorance of the horological industry.

"Hands, creased with courage,
That caress the workbench,
From which springs the fine work—
Behold."

"Voici", 1958, Jacques Brel

Written in La Chaux-de-Fonds, March 2024—LGM

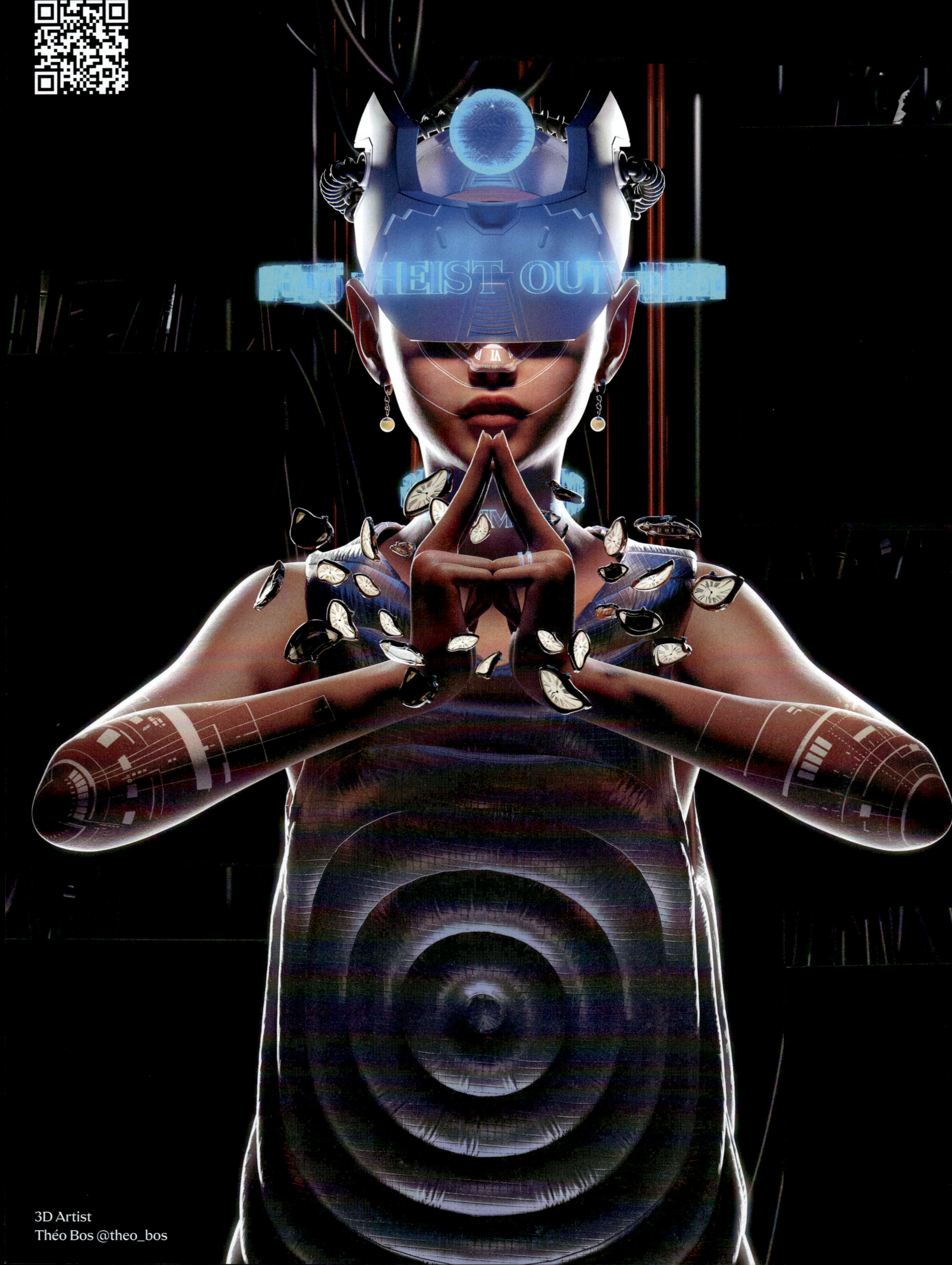

3D Artist
Théo Bos @theo_bos

CARTIER
PARIS

CARTE

Art Director, Photographer, Stylist
Marc-Henri Ngandu
@marc_henri_ngandu

BLANCHE

Model
Samuel Elie (Premium Models)
@samuelelie_

Watches
@otottoi.watches
@marckenrii

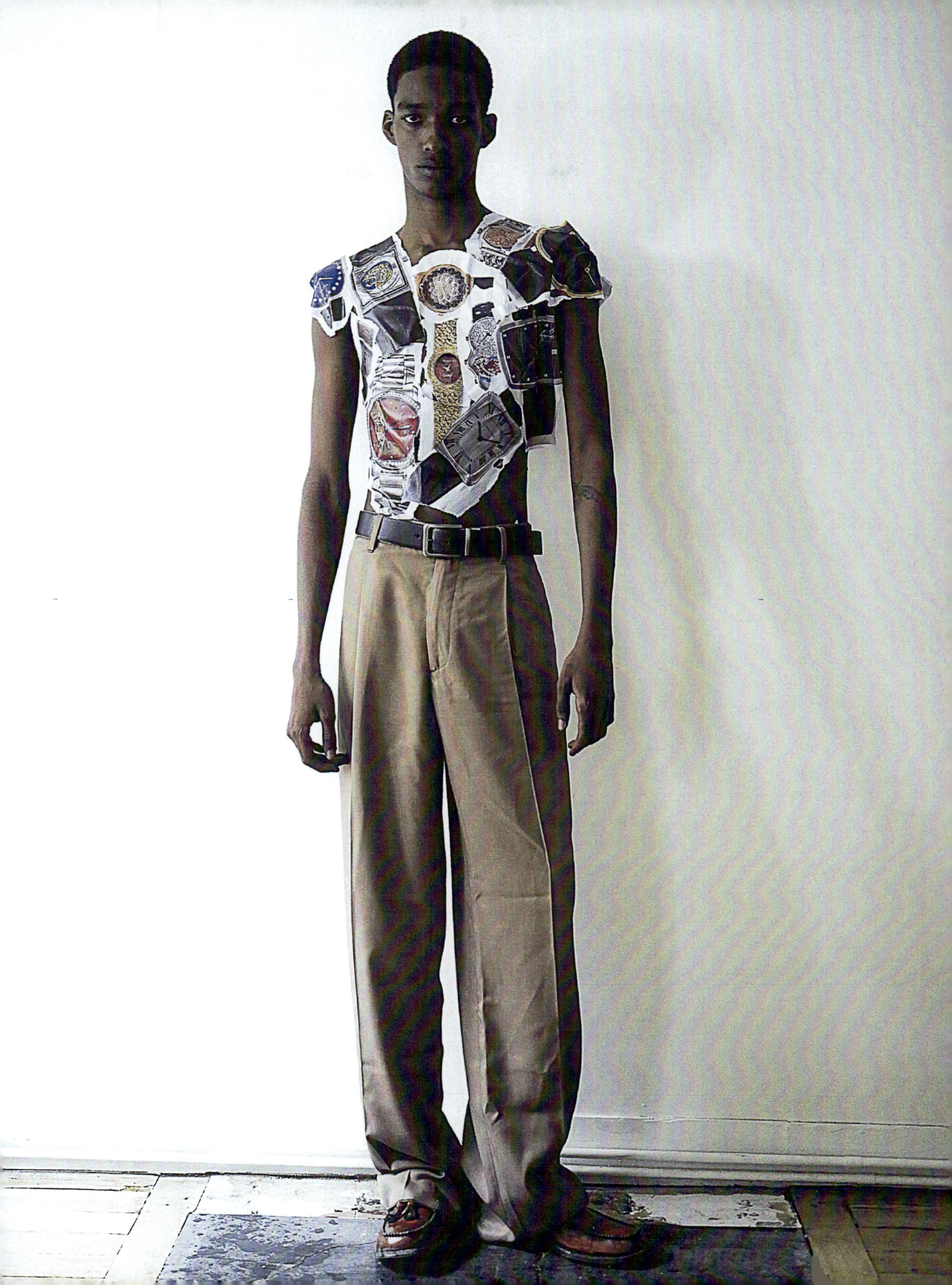

Balenciaga Time Bracelet

LEX
ER
SUPERL
OF
PAR

What's Next

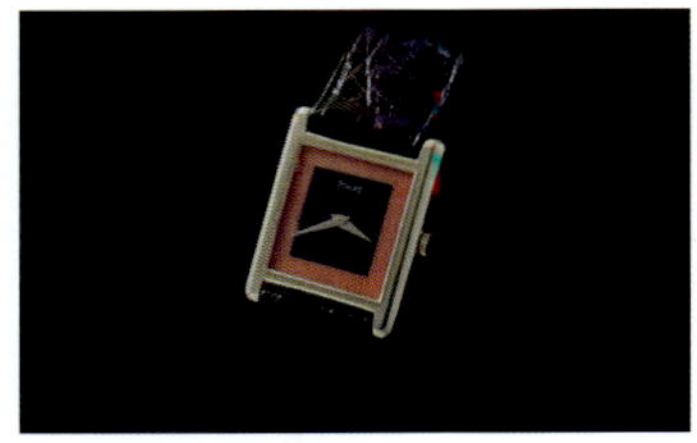

Drawing from my long-term trading experience, recent auction results, and all inquiries from my customers, the watches people are chasing fall into three main categories:

1. My primary focus is smaller-sized dress watches such as the Patek Philippe ref. 96/3796, Cartier Oval, Cartier Baignoire, and iconic models like the Cartier Tank and Santos. I am also keenly interested in the Piaget Tank, Vacheron Jalousie, and the Rolex 6917/69178 Lady Datejust. While these renowned brands and models command much of my attention, I also recognise significant potential in under-the-radar brands like Movado and Corum.
2. I'm also drawn to heftier watch cases that range from medium to substantial sizes but with standout shapes. This emerging trend is undeniably making waves. To clarify, I'm referring to timepieces like the Cartier Bamboo, Cartier Allongée, the oversized Cartier Crash, and from other brands, the Audemars Bamboo, the AP Cobra, and the array of unconventional shapes they've introduced. Additionally, the Patek Philippe Ellipse also falls within this intriguing category.
3. While I hesitate to label it strictly as a "trend," the Rolex Day-Date and Rolex Datejust undeniably hold significant investment and collecting potential. Their extensive variations and combinations offer endless possibilities, mirroring the diverse experiences we encounter daily—meeting new people, delving into new experiences, and constantly expanding our knowledge base.

What binds these pieces together is their exquisite craftsmanship and use of premium materials like yellow gold, white gold, platinum, and rhodium. They frequently showcase sophisticated engine-turned dial finishes—encompassing 'guilloché' pavé de Paris motifs—and stone dials, often paired with diamond baguette indices and gem embellishments. The cases boast intricate designs, ranging from bamboo to braid patterns, while bracelets offer diverse styles like mesh, brickwork, and distinctive motifs, amplifying their innate charm and sophistication. For collectors seeking wise investments, my advice is to zero in on unique configurations—think diamond baguettes mingled with emeralds, sapphires, or rubies. Don't shy away from other rare combinations that may have yet to cross your path.

by Johnson Lee

Biography

In 2010, at just 18, I ventured into selling vintage cameras and lenses. Even during my studies, I was captivated by vintage Rolexes, immersing myself in research and knowledge acquisition despite being unable to afford them at the time. Driven purely by passion, I initially viewed this as a personal pursuit rather than a business endeavour, given my focus was on the camera market. However, after 5-6 years in the second-hand photography sector, I shifted my strategic focus towards horology. Initially juggling both realms, I've now fully immersed myself in the world of watches, into which I channel all my energy and expertise.

@johnson167

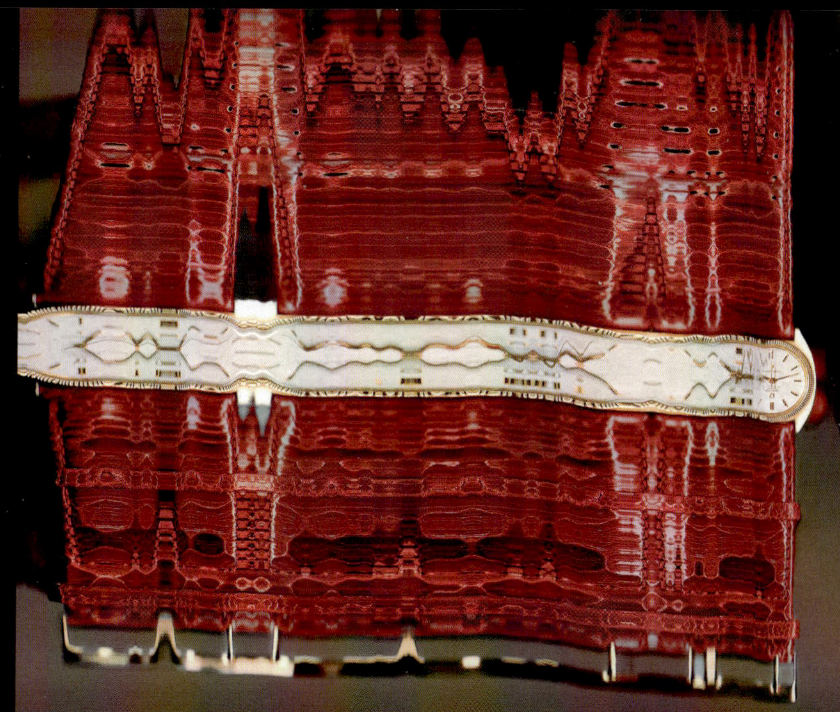

@vildraev

A

B

C

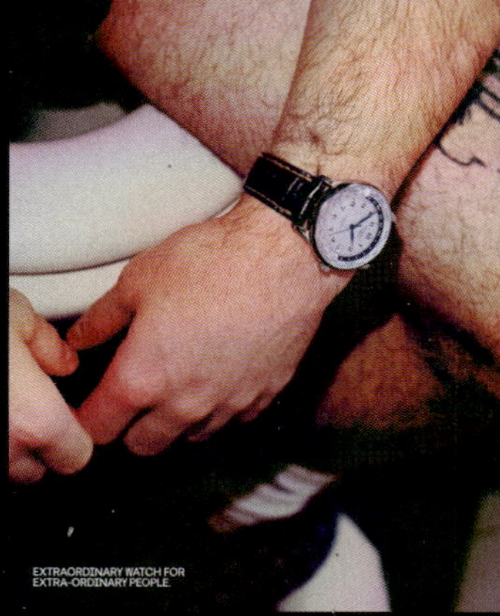

D

E

F

G

Our community
is better than yours

H

I

J

A. @watchesudontsteal B. @joulesmlr/@apolline.deluca C. @kkoobbenn_
D. @bastien.habegger/@mabunator E. @mrnevillewatches F. @mezzer.bvg G. @francescagrima
H. @giuliakai I. @silviogiammarco J. @lotusforrace

A special thank you to

Nour Karam, Sophie Satorre, Laura Marino and Sophie Van Houten from Audemars Piguet, Serge Maillard from Europa Star, Aurélie Streit & Pascal Ravessoud from FHH, Thery Couturier from hic & nunc, Silvio & Flavio from Nardi, Mike Wolf, Andrea Furlan & Laure Michel from Furlan Marri, Nick Marino & Bruno Barba from Sotheby's, our beloved Harris Skandalakis from Mendel Watches, Thaddé Comar, Héloïse Le Plomb, Julien Bon, Elias Marte, Rejjie Snow, Arthur Pfister, Lara Shapiro, Aydrian Ryan Cook, Sofija Zarubica, Hristijan Zheznovski, Hugo Lecot, Vincent Deschamps, Motoki Nakatani, Scarlett Baker, LGM, Théo Bos, Marc-Henri Ngandu, Alexandre Gouverneyre, Lara Shapiro.

9

The magazine owes its existence to the genius and extremist graphic designer, Valentin Vitus. Without him, it simply wouldn't exist. Rémi Le Plomb and Paul Chevalier for their dedication and support throughout the project. Emmanuel de Montbron for proofreading and translating this mag with passion. Guillaume Ferrand for this one-of-a-kind poster artwork. A huge asscheek kiss to all our CheniboyZ for their support, humour and creativity. Harris Skandalakis, Joel Laplace, Alessandro Fanciulli, Arthur Pfister, Thery Couturier, Nicolas Amsellem, Dahl Brunel, Julien Bon, Yoni Krissi, Antonio Vespoint and Scarlett Baker our one and only CheniGirl. To Barbara Sampaio for her unconditional love, patience, and support <3 Lorenzo Maillard. To Pauline, without you there is no me, no magazine. To Georgia, I've been wearing our little bracelet all along I promise <3 Maxime Couturier.

SERICA
All they needed to be on time
was a Serica Chronometer
08h30 PARIS LATE
08h51 NICE LATE
09h24 MARSEILLE LATE
09h36 STRASBOURG LATE
09h40 LYON LATE
09h47 ANGERS LATE
09h52 NANTES LATE
09h55 RENNES LATE
10h11 ST-ETIENNE LATE
10h17 SERICA ON TIME
10h23 GRENOBLE LATE
10h28 BESANÇON LATE
10h34 TOULOUSE LATE
10h42 LILLE LATE
CHRONOMÈTRE
200m = 660ft
355
326
32 rue de Turenne
Paris

Index

GRA
GRAGO
GRAGO

AGO
GRAGO
GRAGO
GE·106 760

Bob McTalksalot
Online

What's the difference between automatic and mechanical watches?

Is there any difference between a tourbillon and a carousel?

Is every chronograph considered a chronometer?

Is "Swiss Made" genuinely Swiss?

How long do I need to check my wrist to rewind my watch?

Are there any good watch educational pages to follow?

Is a tiger eye dial made from an actual tiger's eye?

...

Ask the experts!

CULTURE BY FH
WATCHES

heist-out

Votre message...

THE NEXT
FURLAN
MARRI
WILL
BE
A
FURLAN MARRI

"Where It All Began"

Photographer
Basile Deschamps
@basile.deschamps

Assistant
Tristan Deschamps
@t.ofield

Balthasar de Pury

Welcome to Val-de-Travers, my dear readers; a place seemingly untouched by time, immune to the craze of modernity. Here, the raw nature and its abrupt climate soothe the overstimulated nerves of a society racing against itself; a return to the roots with its fields, its forests, its wildlife, its silence. It's a sort of pilgrimage, even for those who lack spirituality. An exercise in contemplating simplicity.

Today, I'm with heist-out, who thought it a brilliant idea to trek to the farm a month before its official opening so you could read this article in time. They have no idea how rough the climate can be here in the Swiss Jura, the cradle of watchmaking, far removed from their usual haunts in Roma, Paris or New York, where they drink negronis with fancy people at posh parties financed by luxury conglomerates. Val-de-Travers perfectly embodies the watchmaker's ethos: humility, hard work, dedication, an inseparable bond to their land. A stark contrast to some of their creations' wearers, living in the glitz and wearing a watch for status only because, unfortunately, they can't sling their supercar over their shoulders.

The farm, while unfortunately not livable in winter, was built 250 years ago by an ancestor (Abram de Pury, Lieutenant Colonel of the armed militias of the Val-de-Travers) and meant for summer use, as it tends to be chillier inside than out. It's perfect for a natural cool during heatwaves, but come winter, it's a freezing no-go. Thanks to global warming, I can stay a bit longer every year, but at the expense of my pine trees, slowly succumbing to death. My friend Claude-Alain Bugnon, absinthe producer & ex-moonshiner, jokes that he's the first economic casualty of climate change in the area as I extend my stay each summer, drinking his absinthe for free.

OMEGA
WEARNES

They offer you a glimpse of the past, showing you things most brands are incapable of doing today. You see, post-quartz crisis, financial entities stepped in (I have to give them credit for salvaging what was left of the watch industry when even the Swiss Confederation had given up), but their contemporary mantra is faster, cheaper, reducing our cherished timepieces to just another mass-market commodity. Profit is king, whether we're talking condoms or canned tomatoes.

Now let's talk about pocket watches, what's not to love about them?

Art Deco pocket watches are the quintessence of watch design, laying down the aesthetic codes of contemporary watchmaking. If you're into wristwatches, think of these as the same but heftier. What I'll often hear from status wearers is "Yeah, but you can't wear it". Well, who cares? Most of your watches are locked away in safes anyway.

The material contrast and textural harmony showcase such perfect balance, penned by those who defined Art Deco—a style inextricably linked to the Sapin Style born in La Chaux-de-Fonds. Each numeral has been carefully designed to fit seamlessly into the dial. And damn, that printing quality! The dials of the finest watchmakers today look like redials from Latin America in comparison.

And the cases, those flawless step cases that seem to lead you to the Garden of Eden. Devoid of open casebacks, the in-house movements, masterfully decorated, weren't for the world to see, but for the watchmakers to admire and be baffled by the work of their forerunners. Today, we exhibit soulless machine-finished movements with edges so sharp they will give you tetanus.

Back in the day, the watchmaker alone decided when his timepiece was complete, not someone with a background in windshield wipers. No marketing, no ambassadors, no bullshit—just a labour of love and passion.

But the quest, my friends, is much tougher than finding the Albino Yeti, especially for a half-OCD like me, who can only tolerate flawless 'bonbon' condition pieces produced in very small numbers and sometimes unique. And let's not forget that WWII occurred in between, and most of them ended up buried beneath the rubble in occupied territories. The ecstasy of uncovering a chalice is sensational, but it's a rare phenomenon that only occurs a few times a year.

17

The bunker

Tucked away in the woods, a mere 10 minutes from the farm, stands a bunker built during WWII to counter a potential German invasion and expanded during the nuclear paranoia of the Cold War.

I'll never forget the call I received from the Swiss Army asking me if I would be interested in purchasing it. After a year of procedures and promises never to drink any booze within its walls, I was handed the keys. We promptly smuggled in some illicit absinthe, and it quickly became a must-see attraction for any visitor. The only tricky part, especially after the fourth glass, is when you need to break the seal and climb up the 5-meter ladder to answer nature's call. And don't mind the mutant spiders that have never seen daylight: their bite won't turn you into Spiderman.

The glacière

A natural phenomenon of crevices cools the air and turns the 'glacière' into an eternal stock of ice. Even during the scorching heatwave, you will find some ice in the pit. In the 19th Century, the ice cave's frozen water was sent to Paris by train to cool the bottles of absinthe during the Belle Époque. (Parisians would drink up to 30 million litres every year). My cousin used to go there to trip on magic mushrooms that he had picked on cow dung; quite a bold move, considering the 32-meter ditch somewhere in the glacière.

Chrétien Guillaume de Lamoignon de Malesherbes, the lawyer of Louis XVI, visited the glacière during his trip to the Val-de-Travers. It was his last one as he unfortunately lost his head after returning to Paris to defend the king. "Your sacrifice is so much the more generous, that you will expose your own life, and you will not save mine," Louis answered him.

The fire

One of my biggest pleasures in life is to light a fire. It always reminds me of when my brother and I were boy scouts and had been tasked with keeping the campfire burning all night. We failed miserably, succumbing to sleep and missing out on our badges. Since then, I have taken my revenge, becoming a master firemaker, concocting exquisite dishes in 19th-century cast iron pans (the smokiness gives such a unique taste to even the simplest dishes) and keeping them alight for Witches' Sabbath in the company of the green fairy until early morning, when the farmer's return signals the curfew.

18

Now you understand, my dear readers, my lust for ticking devices with a soul and why I won't be seen in the dark corners of Geneva in summer. But legend has it that if you call my name three times in the enchanting woods of Val-de-Travers, I may appear with a drink to quench your thirst.

Balthasar De Pury

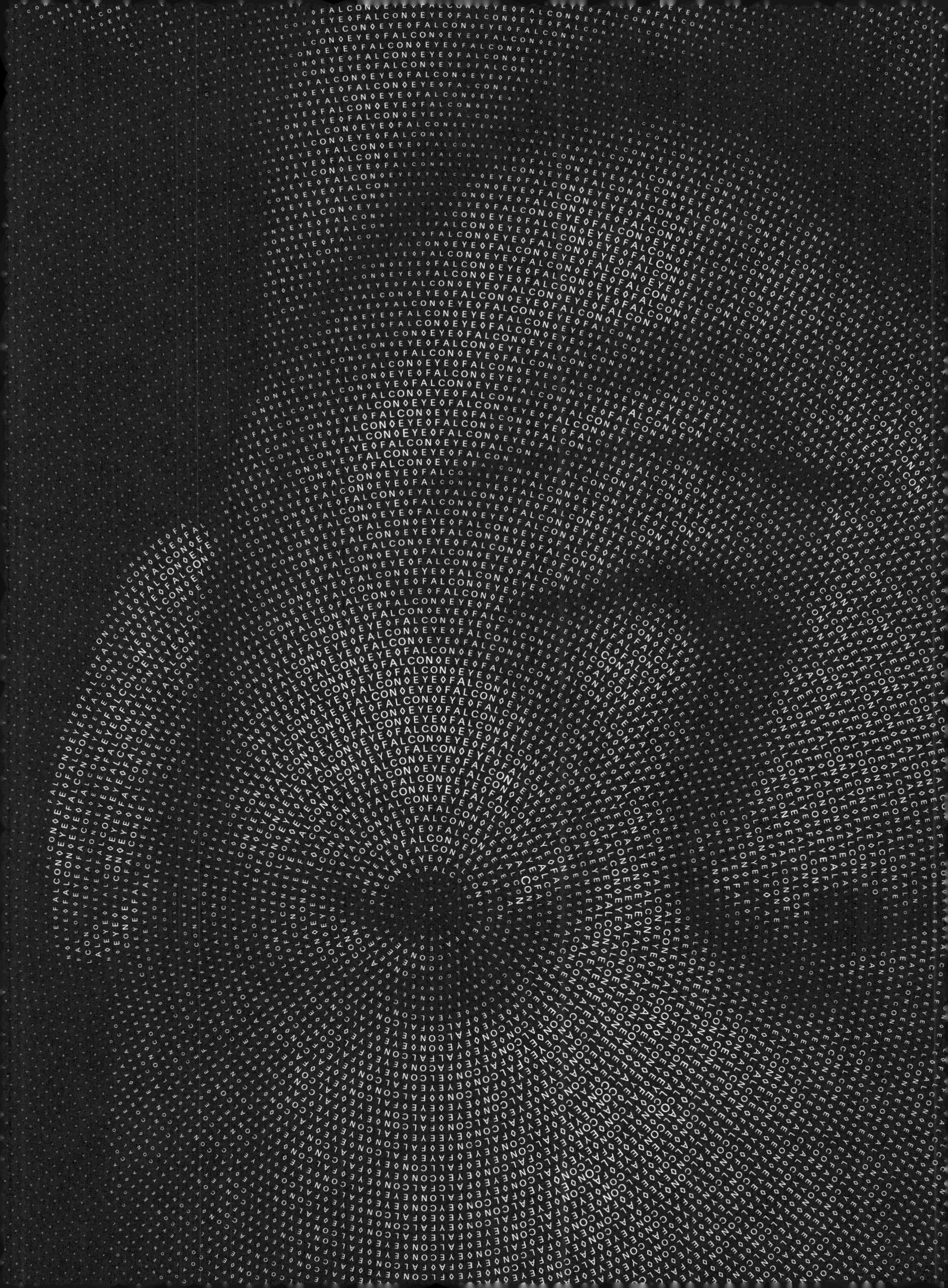
FALCON◊EYE

The Falcon Eye
Alain Borgeaud, Piaget Head of Patrimony
interviewed by Alessandro Fanciulli @mr.a

Alain, we're thrilled to have a chance to sit and talk with you. Today, we want to get to know you a little better, understand where you come from, and what resonates with you. We're keen to dive into your collection and glimpse the world through your eyes.

Alain Sure! I'll start by saying that I am not a watchmaker by trade. My realm has always been the heart. I work with emotions.

Mr. a Could you trace your journey back to where it all began?
Alain After obtaining my A Levels, I joined the Jewellery section of the Decorative Arts school in Geneva, where I graduated in 1986. My early days were spent in ateliers that specialised in the creation, repair, and transformation of watch-related pieces... One atelier in particular had deep links with Piaget. So, before I even knew it, I was already tied to the brand. Yearning to dedicate myself to jewellery, I soon left this watch-focused atelier and joined another atelier owned by the cousin (Denise) of Jean-Claude Gueit, an emblematic designer who worked closely with Valentin Piaget and many other brands including Rolex, Patek, Delaneau, Vacheron to mention a few. Jean-Claude Gueit is credited as the designer of the original Piaget Polo and the Baume et Mercier Riviera. At the time, the Cartier/Vendôme group was looking to buy an atelier specialised in prototyping. We were the perfect match. Early every week, we had designers coming in with fresh drawings and ideas, and by Friday, the prototypes would be ready. I remember the day Alain-Dominique Perrin came to visit. We made sure everything was set properly and after his visit we heard we had been bought. Thus after purchasing Piaget in 1988, the now-Richemont group bought us in 1989, marking the beginning of my involvement within both.

Mr. a What aspect of jewellery-making attracted you to the craft?
Alain I'm a manual guy. I need to touch and feel. I would buy jewellery items from shops, take them apart and put them back together to understand their construction. I've always been driven to create, to express my inner voice.

Mr. a So, why Piaget...?
Alain I was born a Jeweller and that is why I fell in love with Piaget. It was the perfect match.

Mr. a Tell us about your journey at Piaget.
Alain I initially spent 10 years at Piaget's manufacturing department until I reached a juncture where I yearned for evolution. I also had in mind leaving the bench and moving into a more business-oriented position. When I heard the Van Cleef and Arpels 'chef de projet' was leaving, I jumped on the occasion. Shortly after, the blueprints for the "trapeze homme" were in my hands: it was the world's most expensive watch at the time. I remember vividly: it was the 15th of June, and we were told that by the 19th of September, this masterpiece had to be in the client's hands at Place Vendôme in Paris, or it would be declined. The pressure was palpable. Funny enough, the assembly took place at my former atelier, with the watchmakers coming in from La Côte-aux-Fées to collaborate with the jewellers. Together, they invested a full day to assemble the watch... I will never forget that day.

Interesting... So, there was a very intimate relationship between the jeweller and the watchmaker. Do you believe it endures today?

Alain Indeed, these are two very distinct types of savoir-faire that magically intertwine... Remember, back in the day, there were two separate divisions for jewellery and watchmaking in the company. Today they have merged into one company and there is a strong desire to coalesce them into a more coherent and unified entity.

Mr. a On to personal preferences: leather strap or golden bracelet?
Alain Of the eight pieces in front of us, more than half have a golden bracelet... Piaget's reputation in this arena has always been excellent since the 1960s. The company kept buying plenty of ateliers to ensure the highest level of manufacturing. It sometimes feels like wearing a second skin.

Mr. a Do you have a favourite material?
Alain I love yellow gold. Its warmth is unparalleled.

Mr. a Ah yes... I can relate to the love of gold... When it comes to watch movements, what is your take on quartz?
Alain Well, one of the first watches I bought was quartz, and though my preference may have shifted towards mechanical watches over time, I still acknowledge the comfort and technical innovation inherent in quartz movements. Take, for example, this Piaget Polo ref. 7131 (A), its 7P calibre was 35 times more accurate than any comparable quartz movement of its era. And it was the slimmest movement around at the time! Let's remember that back then, it was so chic that we signed dials 'Piaget Quartz' because the company was proud of it... and it allowed Piaget to succesfully navigate the quartz crisis.

Mr. a Now, onto something we all love: what are your favourite stone dials?
Alain Falcon Eye, especially when paired with white gold. I'm also captivated by pristine blue, inclusion-free lapis-lazuli... I'm not a fan of tiger's eye, it's too yellow for me, and onyx is a little too 'hard' on the eye, too... I'm also fond of jasper and its typical red, blood-like inclusions.

Mr. a Could you encapsulate your role at Piaget?
Alain Officially I am in charge of Piaget's legacy. Part of my job spans curating, completing, and most of all, propagating our collection. In collaboration with Benjamin Comar, we've infused a dynamic rotation of iconic models within our flagship boutiques. However, as you can imagine, it's not enough to merely distribute the watches... It's about endowing each timepiece with a particular narrative and context. In two years, I will retire, so my most important mission now is to transmit the love of this brand and all that I've learned for the past thirty years.

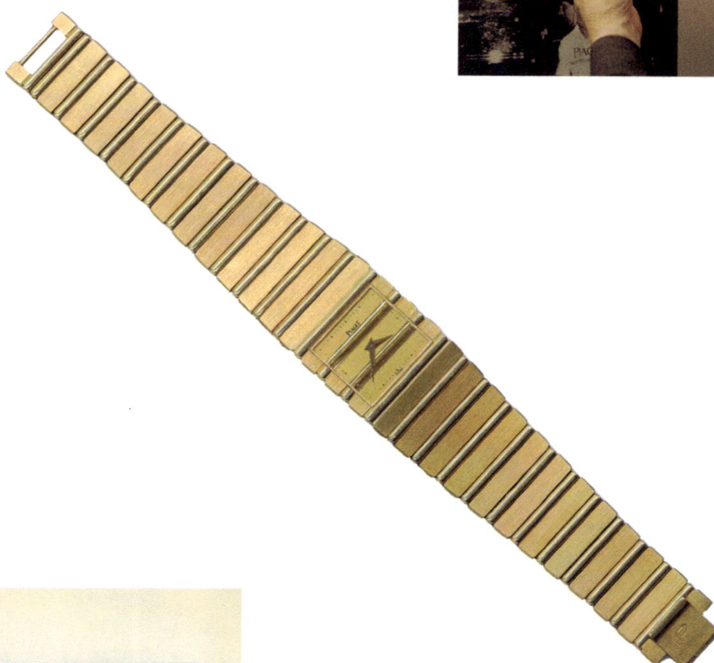

Mr. a Is there a potential clash between your personal collection and Piaget's?
Alain Well, Piaget invariably holds the priority, ensuring no conflict arises. Currently, the museum's collection is pretty complete. We're only yearning for outrageously unique watches. Although I have to confess that our selection criteria converge when it comes to choosing a watch: extra-thin movements, vibrant colours, and a dash of extravagance... I guess what I'm missing now in my personal collection is a gem-set piece.

28

29

Mr. a So why do you think we, as a young generation of passionate watch lovers, should look into Piaget?
Alain It's an audacious and generous brand, one that has brilliantly tied two universes: jewellery and watches. The details speak for themselves. The amount of effort that went into the smallest of elements... Their creations are often genuinely unbelievable. Take a look at this piece [A]. Look at how they decided to integrate these perfectly shaped strips of onyx in the dial of this model 9131 to mimic the empty spaces of the bracelet. Isn't it incredible? Creatively, the brand is on another level.

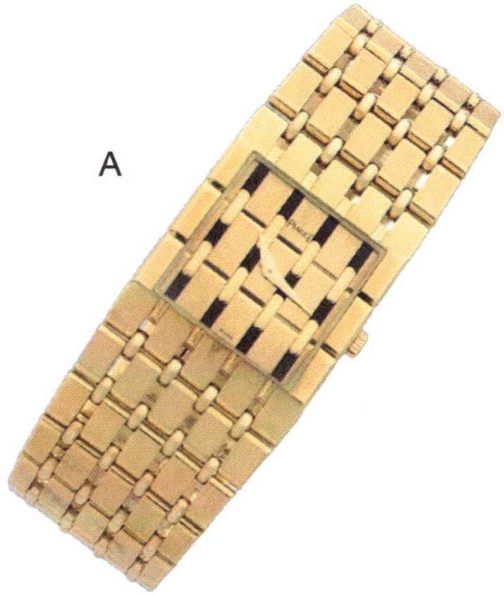
A

Mr. a Do you still discover new pieces, and is there anything particular you are looking for in a watch?
Alain Absolutely, I'm always keen to discover new pieces... I recently came across a jade and lapis-lazuli manchette that blew me away! I'd never seen anything quite like it. We constantly scour for «Parures» a.k.a comprehensive jewellery sets of historical significance, including a necklace, earrings, and a matching pendant or watch for our Private Collection. These unique sets were treasured for their rarity and lineage to nobility, which means they seldom hit the market.

Mr. a Your top two picks from the Piaget Collection?
Alain The first is a gem that's not the priciest but exudes femininity. It's a precursor to the gala with its integrated white gold bracelet, marquise-cut diamond set bezel and lapis-lazuli dial. Only eight pieces exist. I remember a friend had an opportunity to buy one not too long ago for only 4,000 CHF—a steal! Unfortunately, by the time I found out, it was too late—the piece was sold! Let's say our estimation is closer to 50,000, so yes, it's a pity.
The second one would be a masterful manchette with gold wire braids and a captivating, shell-like tiger-eye dial shape that you can basically wear both ways. It's truly incredible, and one of the most exquisite goldsmithing works I have seen.

Mr. a What is your sentiment on the market today? Have you noticed any shifts in trends?
Alain I tend not to delve into market trends... I couldn't tell what different demographics are precisely looking for and why. But Piaget has always remained true to its signature style and tradition, setting its own trends—a reason why people have always been drawn to the brand and always will. It sets you apart from the rest.

Mr. a Any other passions you pursue?
Alain I love contemporary art, travelling, listening to music, photography and, of course, good food!

Mr. a Your ideal daily trip?
Alain A jaunt to Venice, ideally during the Biennale. I would leave Lausanne with the first train, visit the Arsenale, which blows me away every time, have lunch, walk around and return just in time for the last train. A perfect day.

Mr. a And what would you listen to during the trip?
Alain Maria Callas, of course!

Mr. a Favorite Movie?
Alain 'Les enfants du paradis' from 1945. A must-see. Visual poetry at its purest.

Mr. a Favorite Colour?
Alain Lapis-lazuli blue.

Mr. a Has Mr. Piaget seen your personal collection?
Alain Yes, sure… and he was very enthusiastic about it! He's always valued that Piaget's ethos is embraced by its people. I recall the speech he gave at his wedding, celebrating the people close to him who 'think' and 'live' the Piaget way. It was his way of expressing that Piaget is more than a brand, it's a way of life. And I think that's beautiful.

Mr. a Impressions on the new Polo79?
Alain It's nothing short of amazing. This watch resonates with people in such a genuine way. I have been blown away by people's joyful reactions when they see it, especially the pure, spontaneous reactions of those who might not be so knowledgeable about watchmaking but 'feel' the significance of the piece.

Mr. a Do you miss the manual work?
Alain I do, every day. That's why, when I retire, I plan to move into a bigger apartment, set up a little atelier, and start creating. My first piece will be a ring because I love them.

Mr. a Where do you see the future of Piaget?
Alain There is a vision and a willingness to focus on the pillars of the brand: extravagance, ultra-thinness, and colour. Everyone understands these qualities, yet some of them are subjective so it's always a challenge to find the right expression. At the same time, the brand is becoming more self-conscious of its true potential. The focus seems to be shifting back towards leveraging these unique attributes, supported by clear strategic choices. This, to me, is the pivotal aspect of our vision of the future.

Mr. a Are we losing the metal bracelet savoir-faire?
Alain In the 1970s, I counted 104 different metal straps and finishing styles. By the end of the 1980s, the trend shifted towards leather straps or less complex styles, so it's only natural that we lost some artisans along the way. However, we are resolutely steering back towards this art form, and Piaget is investing to keep this tradition alive.

B

Mr. a Is there a particular metal bracelet design that resonates with you?
Alain Probably this one [B]. I love the masculine, chain-like structure and the attention to detail that went into it. Notice the angled polish along the edges, which works perfectly with the overall satin finish. It's this manufacturing perfection that makes me love these watches. What is most interesting to note is that the construction type of this specific bracelet in the reference system is known as 'A' (a letter you see stamped in the reference). What this means is that underneath, all A-type bracelets are structurally the same. Their basic design is identical. However, the magic lies in the finishing—the surface can be adorned with boundless creativity.

Mr. a Ever gifted a Piaget?
Alain Sure, but only to myself! Like this Coin Watch—I was in Venice when you sent me the link, and a few moments later, I bought it. I had to have it.

Mr. a Yes! I knew you were looking for one. Glad it ended up in your collection… Tell us a little bit about it!
Alain The Coin Watch is the ultimate expression of the ultra-thin. Housing the 20P calibre developed by Jean Lassale, this technical marvel was only 1.2mm thick. I love these 'secret' watches. It's the epitome of the protestant-Swiss approach to living in style without exuberance.

Mr. a Finally, could you tell us something crazy that you never would have thought of saying?
Alain I regret not having more arms to wear more watches!

Mr. a Don't we all! Thank you, Alain, it's been an absolute pleasure to sit down and explore your world.

31

Illustrator
Aurélie Ménétrier
@am_illu

the Adventures of HAPPY
the intrepid chamois from Le Brassus

In the heart of the Vallée de Joux, under a mysterious night sky sprinkled with twinkling stars, a special bootcamp for young watch enthusiasts was nestled in the forest. As the moon cast its silvery glow and the campfire flickered, two boys stepped up, eager to share a tale. Gathered around the fire, the children listened intently, ready for a story of bravery and excitement.

The adventures of hAPpy le chamois !

In the serene landscapes of La Vallée de Joux, brave chamois hAPpy roamed the rugged mountainsides with grace and determination. He understood the importance of being bold and taking risks. His long history filled with amazing watch creations shows it, but let's zoom in on the year 1972! This year, with his adventurous heart and the help from watch designer Gérald Genta as well as fellow friends and partners, hAPpy whipped up something fresh, exciting, and game-changing called the **Royal Oak**!

hAPpy and his friends knew the **Royal Oak** design was special, showing strength, bravery, and creativity. With their clever but stubborn mind, they crafted the watch and trusted their guts.

At first, not everyone understood or loved it, but over time, it became a favorite and a special symbol of hAPpy, loved by many!

Sometimes, when you're unique and believe in yourself, you can make magic happen, just like the **Royal Oak** did! So, remember to take chances and dare - it's worth it!

During the magical decade called the 1990s, years after the wondrous **Royal Oak** stole hearts, our adventurous friend hAPpy had a bright idea : a watch perfect for the busy, modern world, but to do that, he knew he had to shake things up again.

hAPpy would often say with a mischievous grin :

With the help of the wizard watch designer, Emmanuel Gueit, they set to work. Together, they turned the **Royal Oak** into a watch that was tougher and sportier than ever before. Inspired by speedboat races, they named it the **Royal Oak Offshore**. And because of its big, bold size, some even gave it a special nickname - «The beast».

Once again, crafting this special watch was no easy feat. When hAPpy and Emmanuel unveiled their creation, some people, including some collaborators, thought it was too bulky and heavy at 250 grams ! In simple terms, many felt it was just too bold and hefty !

But, oh ! With hearts full of hope and a stubborn sparkle, hAPpy and Emmanuel held tight to their dreams. Little by little, people began to see the magic and wonder of this special watch. And so, their dreamy creation found its way into the hearts of many, proving that belief and determination can make anything possible !

Fast forward to 2019. The legendary octagonal shape of the **Royal Oak** had captured countless hearts. Everywhere you turned, people chattered about it : « Octagon here, Octagon there ! » Now, our friend hAPpy, though a bit more experienced, still had that mischievous twinkle in his eye. He was ready to stir up a new adventure ! With a playful idea in mind, he introduced **CODE 11.59** to the world.

First, the name **Code 11.59**, was inspired by the last minute before time flits to a new day. It hinted at the excitement of a brand-new day and a big hug to the future ! However, this time, hAPpy faced a challenge as big as a mountain ! He had to create a watch collection that celebrated tradition yet spoke to the young, spirited watch-lovers of today.

Everything had to be different and daring : 13 new models and 6 calibers, a brand-new round case sprinkled with tiny octagonal hints, and a magical panoramic glass that seemed to disappear !

To tackle this colossal challenge, hAPpy rallied his talented friends from all corners of Switzerland. As hAPpy often said, « Believing in your dreams is important, but believing in the people who help you chase them is even mightier ! » Lucas Raggi, the mad scientist and R&D director, chuckled as he recalled some of the funny hurdles they faced. At first, some playful critics whispered that the **Code 11.59** was too different from the beloved **Royal Oak**.

But for our lively little chamois, hAPpy, this wasn't a new melody. With dedication and teamwork, a special milestone was reached. 4 years later in 2023, the **Code 11.59** was truly celebrated for what it was, a marvelous collaboration effort. It brought to life the Ultra-Complication Universelle RD#4 model with 40 functions of which 23 were magical features, earning the coveted Aiguille d'Or award.

As the night grew still, stars twinkled brighter. It was time for the young watch enthusiasts, their eyes full of wonder, to settle into their sleeping bags, drifting into dreams under the starry sky.

Above them, hAPpy the Chamois twinkled among the stars, a gentle protector of dreams and daring adventures. He reminded them that trusting your instincts is key, but leaning on the guidance of positive friends can help you soar even higher, all while staying true to where you started !

Help hAPPy the chamois in crafting his next masterpiece! Imagine and sketch the most fantastical watch you can dream up. Grab your pencils and start drawing it just underneath!

Operation Enduring Freedom For Your Wrist

Lorenzo Maillard

What if I were to ask you the time? Would you glance at your wrist or reach into your pocket? Even though the wrist-check remains a widespread reflex, the latter is steadily gaining favour, a trend likely to intensify with future generations.

Since the early mass-marketing attempts of wristwatches in the first decade of the 20th century, it has taken nearly a century to gradually challenge and modify this ingrained habit of time-checking. While wristwatches dominate hairy and hairless wrists alike (like mine), we often overlook the numerous innovative attempts to reimagine timepiece wear.

Watchmakers thrive on challenges, and when it comes to inventive ways to wear a watch, many have seized the opportunity to propose unconventional yet immensely satisfying ideas. Two distinct periods in the 20th century stand out to me in this regard.

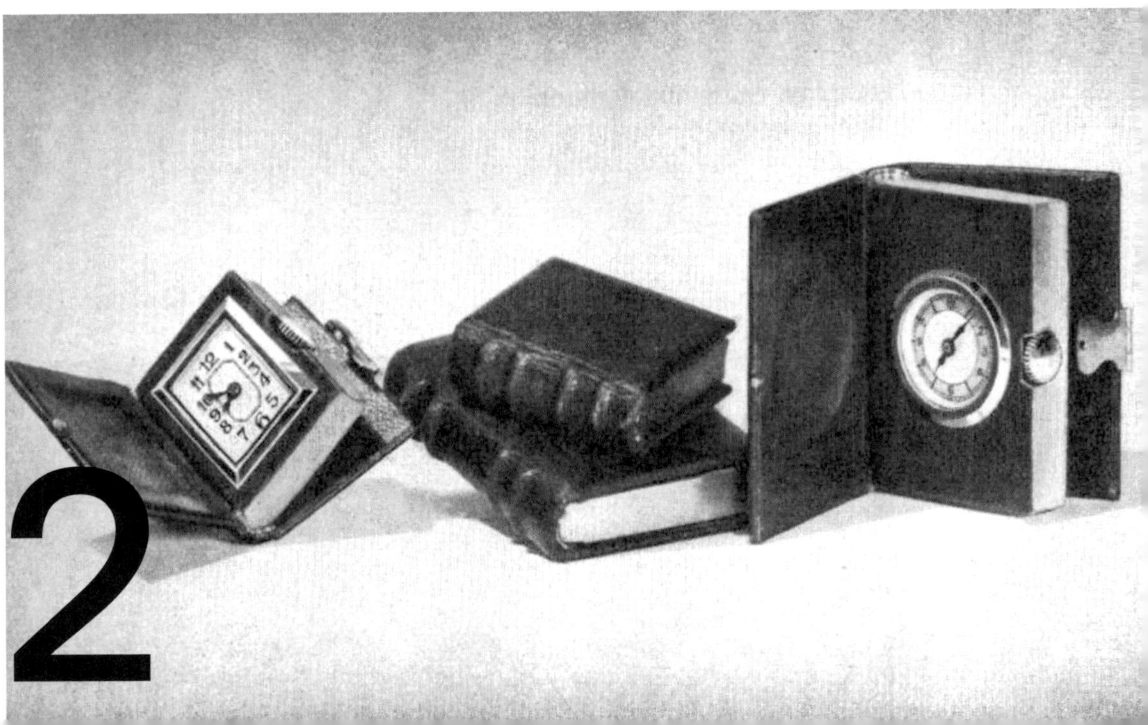

Firstly, the 1930s and '40s—an era I hold dear and consider the epitome of creative watchmaking. This period witnessed a surge in artistic movements, intricate dial designs, unconventional case shapes, stunningly finished calibre, and remarkable miniaturisation. While this age marked the widespread adoption of wristwatches, it also harboured a plethora of inventors eager to defy conventions.

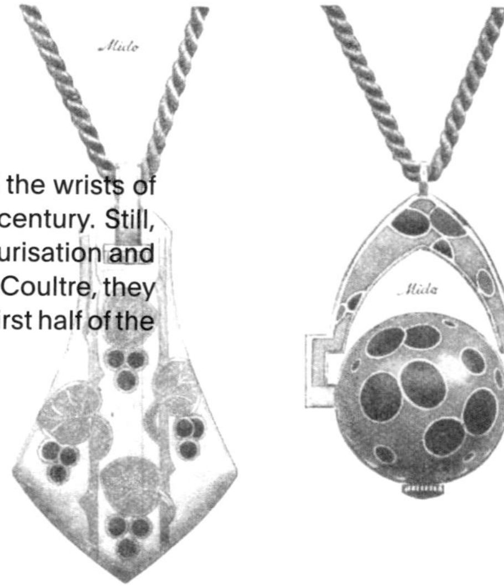

Ring watches had already graced the wrists of privileged individuals in the 19th century. Still, thanks to advancements in miniaturisation and the efforts of brands like Jaeger-LeCoultre, they gained popularity throughout the first half of the 20th century.

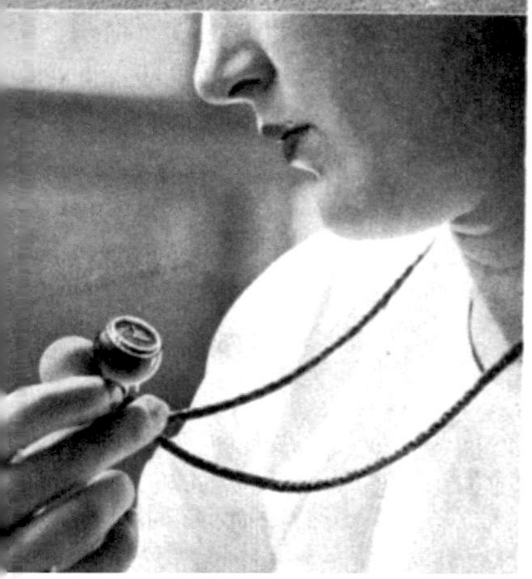

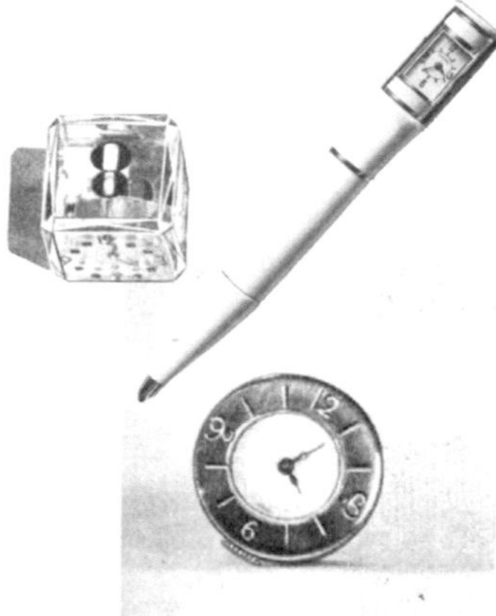

But other watchmakers went further and took the watch entirely out of the arm. Notably, Movado's Ermeto watch deserves mention as a ground-breaking attempt to challenge the dominance of wrist-worn timepieces. Introduced in the early 1930s, the Ermeto was marketed as a chic, self-winding timekeeping accessory that could be attached to jackets, purses, pants, and more. It was among the pioneers of what came to be known as "purse watches." Many brands vied to offer these watches the most ingenious and practical designs.

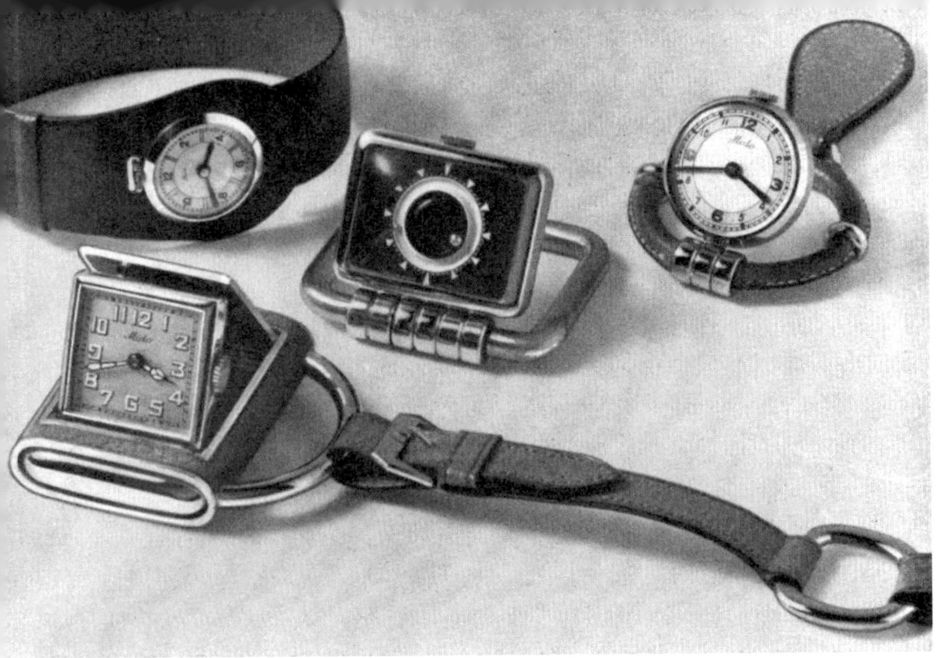

Movado was not alone in this endeavour; Mido and several other brands excelled in devising innovative, portable ways to display the time. Imagine timepieces concealed within golf balls, lighters, dice, animal figurines, keys, belt buckles, coins, chess pieces, miniature books, flowers, or even walnut-shaped watches. While creativity often results in elegant and desirable offerings, it can also lead to questionable design choices. I'll leave that judgment to you.

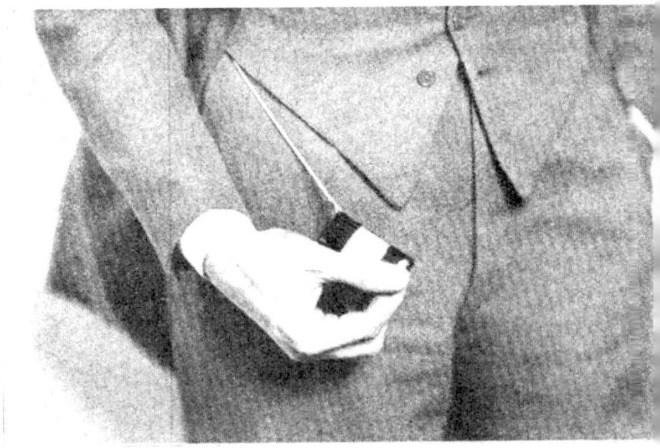

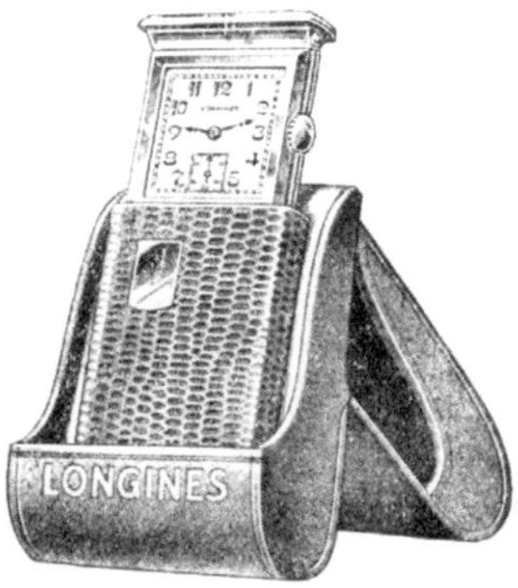

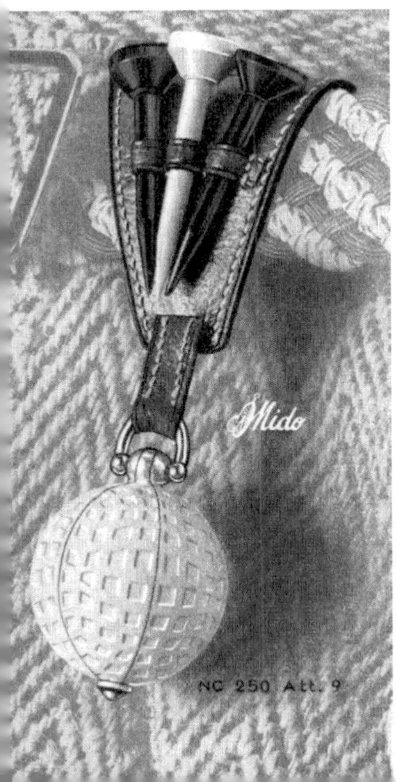

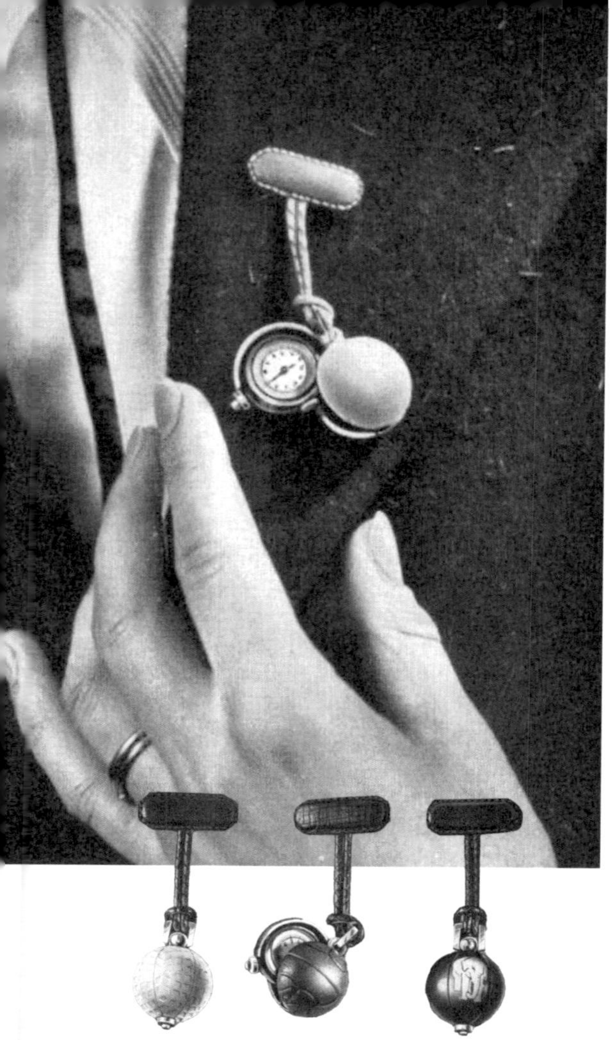

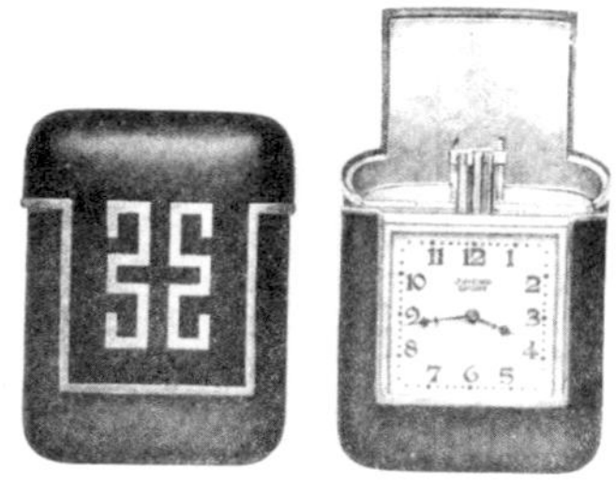

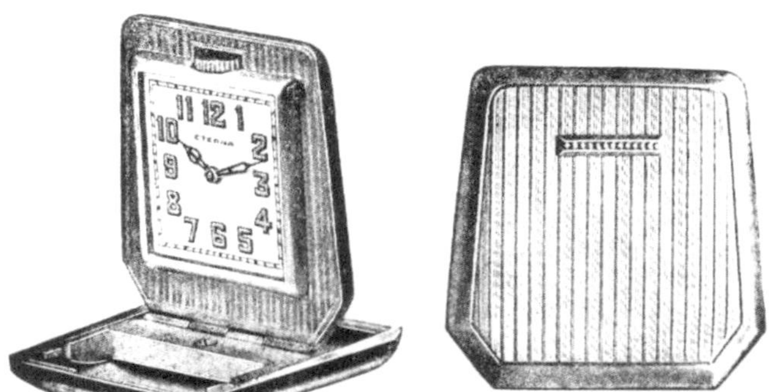

The various efforts to invent new ways of wearing watches further emphasised timekeeping as a fashionable and distinctive means of self-expression. However, this post-World War II surge in inventiveness began to wane as global turmoil escalated, perhaps because the joy and optimism of the interwar period faded amidst the unprecedented atrocities witnessed during the Second World War.

Was it the war's darkness, then? The need for functional "tool watches" tailored for soldiers, doctors, and physicians? Or just the wristwatch's unbeatable practicality?
It's also plausible that, as innovative as these alternative timepieces were, they lacked the practicality of traditional wristwatches. Regardless of the reasons, this once vibrant and expressive inventiveness became increasingly subdued in the watchmaking world by the end of the Second World War.

45

Enter the late '60s and '70s—a playground of unbridled creativity. Maybe it was the LSD discovery (by a Swiss scientist, btw) that sparked imagination, but watchmakers started breaking every rule and exploring uncharted territories... This era birthed a wild fusion of jewellery and watchmaking, producing designs that boggle today's minds.

With various design competitions as the arena, jewellers and watchmakers became rivals in audacity. The result? Pieces that dazzled and some that just left you scratching your head. Picture futuristic, organic shapes straight out of a low-budget sci-fi flick.

Prominent brands such as Piaget, Vacheron Constantin, Patek Philippe, Audemars Piguet, as well as lesser-known names like La Montre Royale, Bueche Girod, Delaneau, and Schlegel & Plana, all embraced a similar approach. Their creations boasted the lavish use of gold, precious stones, and hard stones, showcasing impeccable craftsmanship. These groundbreaking designs would not have been possible without the visionary input of designers like Gilbert Albert, Andrew Grima, Augustin Plana, and Charles de Temple, among others.

These innovative timepieces transcended traditional forms, manifesting as rings, necklaces, pins, brooches, and even clocks. Some ventured into the realm of luxury fashion items, with some pieces ingeniously incorporated into bags or jackets.

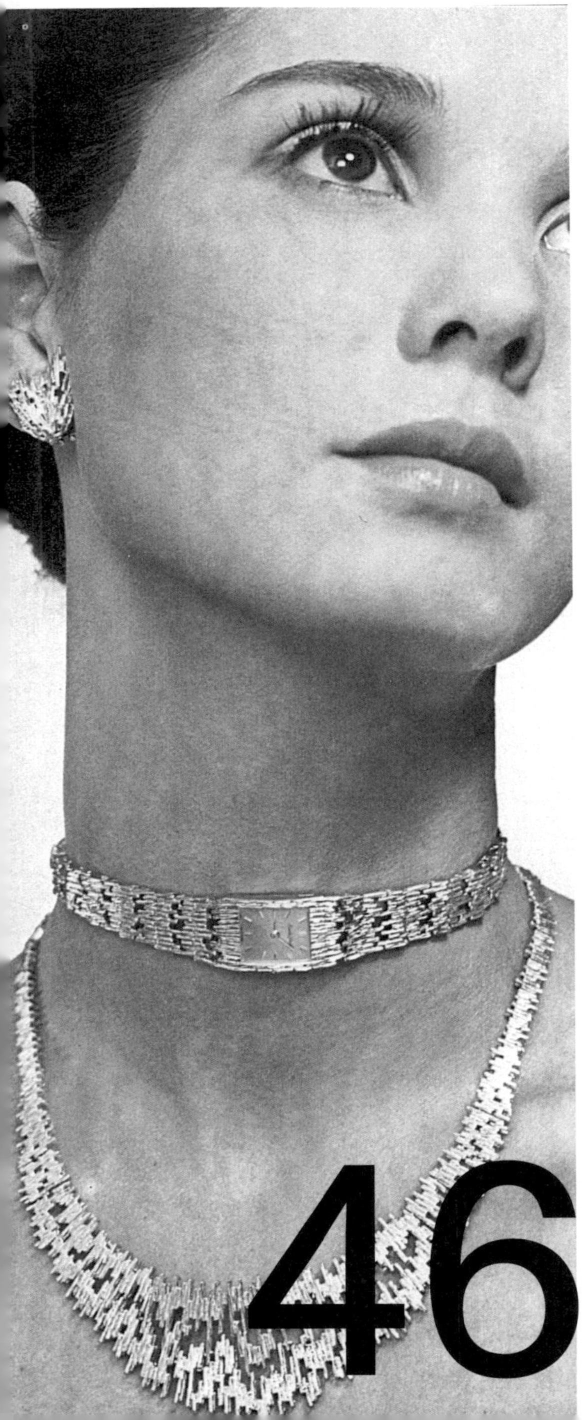

46

Think Rihanna pioneered the watch choker trend? Think again. Early 1970s editorials depict models flaunting watch chokers. The adage holds true: "We never truly invent; we simply resurrect what was once deemed passé."
Wearing your watch around your neck is probably a clever way to dodge the "what time is it?" question. The only snag? You'll never be able to read it yourself!
On the flip side, some brands got playful but strayed into questionable territory—blurring the line between wristwatch and, well, whatever they were thinking.
In this era of boundary-pushing creativity, watches transcended their traditional forms, morphing into lighters, key holders, chains, necklaces, and even pill reminders. That's right—a watch designed to ensure timely medication intake. Whether it was a white vitamin pill or a blue "stimulant," I won't pass judgment, nor should the black-and-white photographs that captured these innovations.

Amidst the quartz crisis and the resurgence of traditional high-end watchmaking, creators shifted from wild, avant-garde designs to more wearable, technically complex timepieces, focusing on complications and the inner workings of watchmaking.

As larger corporate groups with substantial financial stakes took the helm, risk-taking was curtailed, prompting a creative shift towards independent creators. And this couldn't be truer today. While the word 'creativity' is on every brand's lip at watch fairs and in press releases, it feels like we've hit the depths of Mariana's Trench when it comes to bold inventiveness, especially in design. Much like jelly, the less creativity there is, the more thinly it gets spread around.

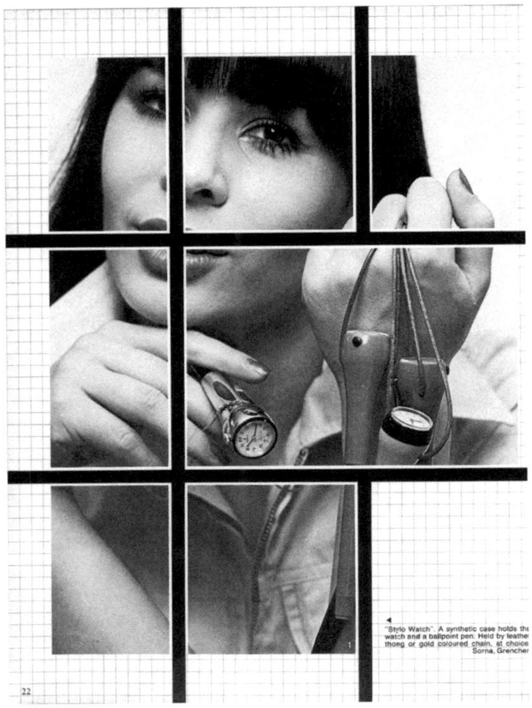

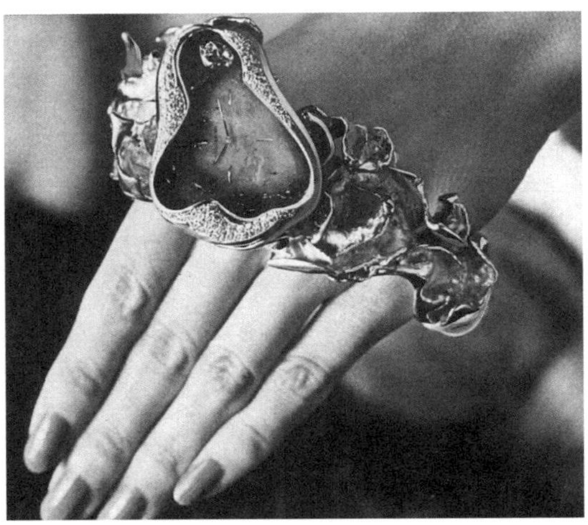

Let's hope the helium escape valve of this over-pressurized industry can release the pockets of creativity and innovation found in independent brands and vintage pieces back to the surface. But we're not there yet...

This year's fair was a prime example. While a handful of brands played their cards right, the majority seemed content to play it safe with animations and collection consolidation. It's high time we added a dash of passion and spice to the mix, crafting a cocktail that might leave you with a hangover, but craving another round. To captivate the next generation of buyers and collectors, the perfect cocktail could resume in a few ingredients: singularity, audacity, and standout products. These will prove fundamental to stay on track.

We're crossing our fingers for a return to those audacious days, whether drawing inspiration from past watchmaking wild ideas or introducing entirely fresh ones. It's high time we saw watches as pure playgrounds for creativity.

That's where the younger generations swoop in to save the day. One thing's certain: in love with products from a long-gone era, today's young watch enthusiasts are going all out to make their mark in the bustling vintage watch arena. They're on a quest for unique pieces that embody their fierce individuality. We've witnessed collectors transition from tool watches to sport-integrated pieces, then to opulent gold and jewellery timepieces, culminating in stone-dial watches. The next frontier? Breaking free from wristwatches altogether and embracing unconventional timekeeping placements on the body.

Some have experimented with ankle-worn watches, waist-mounted timepieces, scrunchies and even shoe-attached watches. Act swiftly, as the body's real estate for watch placement is rapidly dwindling—outside the body, that is.

Now's the perfect moment to shake up how you wear your watch. As watches lose their practical edge, it's high time to let your wrist breathe a little!

Léa Bruneau
@bruneaulea

@sunflowerman

XHEVDET REXHEPI
Minute inerte

Xhevdet Rexhepi: The Young Pope of Hustle Horology
Matteo Maillard

Photographer
Laureat Bakolli
@laureat.bakolli

In the rap game, we all know the Hustler, that legendary figure who rises from nothing, ready to build an empire. He's a self-made 'street' man, tough as sapphire, hell-bent on making it big, regardless of the obstacles. The Hustler typically eyes a spot in music, street hustle, or worse, drugs. But Xhevdet Rexhepi chose hands—watch hands, that is. Not those from Quai 9 or a tattoo parlour, but the ones that tick and tock in timepieces.

On this dreary late afternoon, with a drab sky overhead, we find him steps away from Geneva's station, in his spanking new workshop, with four wooden workbenches in full view from the pavement. A little girl deciphers the name on the luminous shop front like it's a toy store window. "A-te-lier hor-lo-ger," she stutters. No dolls here, just timepieces. "Adult toys," her mother clarifies before pulling her away. Xhevdet, monocle atop his head like a canary-yellow cardigan-clad Cyclops, welcomes us into this bright haven scented with fresh paint. "We haven't quite finished setting up," he exclaims.

Months ago, his horological hustle moved out of the flat he shares with his partner, Teresa, to spread out here. "More space was essential to enter the last phase of pre-production creation." On the benches, his employees Diogo and Louis are bent over the workings of the "Minute Inerte," the moniker for the 33-year-old independent watchmaker's first timepiece. Minute inerte, because his watch's seconds hand pauses. Completing its cycle, the seconds hand stops for two ticks before resuming in sync with the minute hand—a unique technical quirk in mechanical watches. "I wanted to take on the challenge, to create something different, unattempted before," Xhevdet emphasises, his speech punctuated with thoughtful pauses, like

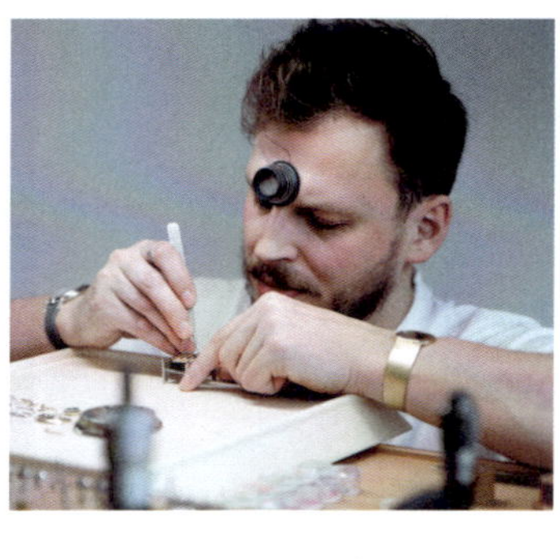

breathers in the relentless race against time. His muse? Clocks in CFF railway stations. Every morning, while waiting for the train at La Plaine near Geneva, on his way to cut his teeth at Patek Philippe, he observed a clock whose seconds hand halted briefly, letting the minute hand catch up before darting forward together. "When I was searching for an original idea for my first watch, I remembered that station clock," he says, adjusting his monocle. "In watchmaking, we often discuss the "dead second," where the hand jumps second to second rather than smoothly gliding. I wanted to shift that concept to the minute. But I dislike the term 'dead,' so I thought of "inerte." It's neither alive nor dead; it's a transitional state before continuation."

Death, which he narrowly escaped at eight, when in 1998, he hastily left his birth village of Zheger in Kosovo amidst the war's crescendo. "Soon after we left, the houses in our neighbourhood were looted and burned." Some family members fled on a tractor to Macedonia, but his father, already living in Switzerland, managed to bring his children over.

The family settled in Lully, rural Geneva. Neither Xhevdet nor his brother Rexhep spoke French, and there were no other Kosovars around. They had to adapt. Integration meant football games with neighbours, where the brothers shone, and school desks, where they quickly picked up the language, customs, and codes. This mentality bonded the siblings. The elder led the way. "While I was apprenticing in cabinetry, Rexhep convinced me to switch to watchmaking." He aced the tests at Patek, got the basics down, and then delved into complications and tourbillons at MHC, now defunct.

Their careers could have coasted comfortably within the industry if the itch for independence hadn't bitten so deep. "It's in our DNA, from father to son!" In 2012, at just 25, Rexhep launched his own watch brand, Akrivia (Greek for 'precision'). It was a bold leap, fraught with risk, that required a rebel spirit and some helping hands. Naturally, he reached out to his brother. "I dropped everything and joined him." The beginnings were tough. They had to pour money into machines and components, not knowing if there would be any return, and building on the hope of future purchases. "In our culture, when your brother starts something, you follow, you support, you hustle, not worrying about whether you'll get paid or not... Debt piled up, but we stayed fixated on our goal."

It's more than 'haute horlogerie'; it's hustle horology! "We had to tighten our belts. There were times we nearly ended up on the streets, the orders not rolling in. Without any safety net, our tenacity grew. We had to forge ahead!" When one brother lost the will to continue, the other was there to rally the spirits. Until that first sale came through. Then, success began to wipe clean their debts. Rexhep was soon able to hire staff beyond his brother. They quickly grew to a team of fifteen. "If we made it, it's because we had no other choice."

With Akrivia on track, Xhevdet dreamt of launching his own brand. By 2020, he was sketching out dial designs and case concepts. Then he remembered those railway clocks, their paused seconds hands, their spoon-like second hands, evoking the sticks of train conductors. In September 2022, he took the leap, leaving Akrivia to launch his own horological venture. It was back to square one. Setting up a workshop, recruiting talent, investing in gear, and self-funding. "It was crazy to start from scratch again, facing those struggles and doubts. I'm beginning to think that's what drives me."

Months of relentless toil later, by July 2023, he was cradling the first prototype of his Minute Inerte. The ancient arches he'd photographed on numerous trips to Rome inspired the dial. A 1930s Ebel pocket watch influenced the case design. Two hundred components breathed life into the movement. "I wanted a watch with classic aesthetics but a disruptive mechanism." A blend of tradition and modernity. A watch enthusiast's dream.

Hunched over their benches, Xhevdet, Diogo, and Louis labour tirelessly to perfect the third prototype. Production is slated to begin in the coming months. Fifty pieces, priced at 83,000 CHF each, are nearly pre-sold, and Xhevdet is itching to dive into the design of two new mechanical timepieces. The details of these future projects are his to keep. Even after a few beers at the Guidoline bar, he's as tight-lipped as ever. "All I can divulge is that the spirit will remain the same. A hearty dose of innovation, a splash of love, and plenty of R&D. I want to experiment with new mechanisms, take risks, and invent—that's where the fun is in this craft!"

His independence is non-negotiable. "Even if someone came knocking with a suitcase full of millions, I wouldn't sell my brand. Money isn't what thrills me. Sure, it's great to have it, to splash out on stuff, but what really gets me going is creating a damn fine watch that people love! Then reinvesting in the next creation, squeezing in some holidays, and I'll be content."
As Booba, the most famed hustler in French rap, might say, "It's kick-ass to be independent."

Flash Questions

What's your main character trait?
Bon vivant. Always upbeat and smiling.
I love a good laugh.

The most beautiful horological creation?
Probably a 1930s pocket watch.

The worst horological creation?
Any watch that's been neglected or is incoherent.

Any brand or watchmaker you'd be keen to collaborate with?
I'd be down to create a watch with Bennahmias or Kendrick Lamar.

Always on time or fashionably late?
Running behind, usually.

What do you do in your free time?
I take time to reflect and sketch.

Where do you see yourself in five hours?
Likely at home, binge-watching a series, probably 'The Last Man on Earth'!

Is time linear or cyclical?
Cyclical.

What happens after death?
Rebirth.

Flija or pizza?
Flija.

Rose gold or sapphire?
Sapphire.

Set or un-set watch?
Sure, why not.

Do you wear quartz watches?
Yes, this one's quartz.
I couldn't stand them before, but I've loosened up.

Do you tell the time by your wristwatch or phone?
On my wrist.

Which app do you use the most?
Instagram.

Which country would you like to live in?
No particular one. Maybe somewhere in southern Europe where it's warm and the food is good, or maybe back in the mountains of Kosovo.

Your greatest achievement?
Being with Teresa and, of course, my watch.

Your biggest regret?
Drifting away from my cultural roots.

Your current favourite song?
Anything by B.B. Jacques.

A song you're embarrassed to admit you like?
"Made in Romania".

Do you have a motto?
No.

What do you want to tell us that you can't say to another magazine?
Fuck Cenovis/"Tu sors ou je te sors"/It's an eye, not a coke spoon.
(choose one of the three)

56

Inner Dialogue Gone Rogue

By Gianfranco Ritschel
www.timetotrain.ch

What? You want to know what's the fuss about this watch? Take a good look at it. No complications. Don't even think about a deep dive! And yes, you'll have to wind it up, even during one of your long-weekend breaks from the rat race. By the way, don't drop it or bang it into something because it's not shockproof. Plus, it bears the battle scars of wear and tear. But you know what? It tells time. That's its gig.

Ashamed of it? Quite the contrary. Let's be honest. This watch has never strutted on the moon, climbed up Mount Everest, braved the abyssal depths, or breezed through a Formula One race. It is technically a total normie, and no celebrity has ever sung its praises or made it a legend.

But you know what? It has survived every fad, all the zaniness, and all the tech revolutions of the past decades. So, why my affection for it? Don't you get it? Skip the search for bells and whistles, because there aren't any. There's no point in making comparisons, it's unique. You can't even measure it, because it is misshapen. And forget the price tag, it was cheap and, by the way, I'm not selling it.

Just keep those eyes of yours peeled! Take in those clean lines that speak of its impeccable balance. Observe the polished facets that reflect the light, seductively winking at us to draw our attention. Bask in the harmony of the smooth, subtle contrasts that highlight the curves and generous surfaces, inviting our fingertips to caress them. It's a sensual, intimate, even meditative interaction.

You're right, maybe I'm a bit nuts! This is my way of loving watches. I can look at one, and let my touch guide my gaze and emotions until I genuinely connect, understand, and maybe even begin to fall in love. At times, we look for some resemblance with familiar visuals, other times, we discern a style, and sometimes, we simply refuse to compare it to anything else. The watch is totally free, it surprises us, and then we simply love it!

Just because the crowd is all in doesn't mean I'm wrong! Indeed! You can love a watch for everything it brings to the table, but you can also cherish it for its pure, undiluted essence. And if some watches try hard to be more and more beautiful, others are simply beautiful.

Cheap is Cool
Antonio Vespoint
Joel Laplace

The assignment is simple and easy: We gave 150 CHF to two of our best watch-hunters from the CheniboyZ and asked them to chronicle their journey. One might have spent it all on wine, but who are we to judge? Too often, watches are pigeonholed as mere investments or pricey objects, yet they have so much more to offer. You don’t need a billionaire’s bankroll to be bitten by the watch bug. The watches we wear most often are usually those with the best stories behind them, not hefty price tags. Enjoy the ride with our two fellow flea-market diggers. We hope you’ll snag a tip or two along the way. And remember, as with everything, the journey prevails over everything else.

150
property of heist-out
150
NATIONAL BANK
OF HEIST-OUT

150
property of heist-out
150
NATIONAL BANK
OF HEIST-OUT

59

Antonio Vespoint
@charmcityjeweler

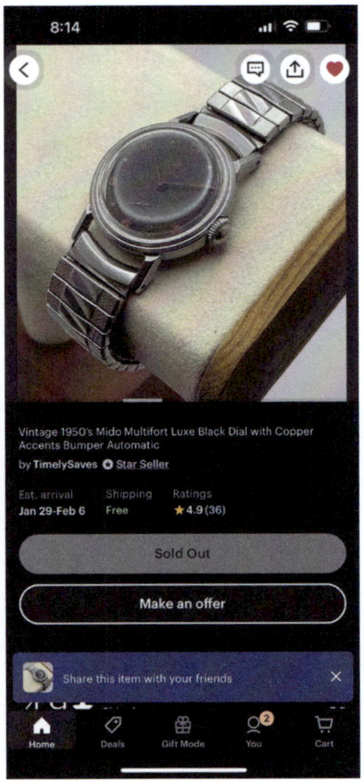

"Here's your assignment. Find a cool vintage watch for 150 Swiss Francs (175 USD) and write about it." M's a straight shooter. He doesn't leave much to interpretation. I like that. Before you get the wrong idea, this IS NOT a "How To" or "10 Tips" rundown. I just want you to hear me out as someone working in the industry who started, as many of us did, as a kid in love with cool watches.

I've always felt that buying in person is superior to buying online. That being said, I sell online, and my local options are a bit slim for my style and for this particular budget. So, I decided to browse the web in an attempt to find something I loved with the funds at my disposal. I mean, that's where everyone buys their watches nowadays, right? "Shit. Why not check 'ol' faithful" There's always something on eBay.

After two nights of feverish, after-work eBay hunting sessions, I Googled "Vintage Watch" and found myself on Etsy. I started typing all my favourite affordable brands into the search bar with a filter showing only the pieces falling below 175 USD.

A few of the pieces that caught my eye all came from one seller. After visiting their page, I realized they had offerings that truly resonated with me but remained invisible to my budget-conscious search. One of these was a black-dial Mido Multifort Luxe in a steel case. I didn't own any black-dial watches (at the time), and the case caught my eye. When hunting for a piece, be it for myself or inventory, I look for something I love. And I loved this one, hands down.

You might wonder what's so special; it's just an aged watch with a faded dial, right? Correct. That's exactly what it is. See, the two things I love about vintage pieces are

their patina and case designs. This one fits the bill. Beyond the piece's plausible originality, its unique patina gives each dial a distinctive look. Patina showcases how the piece has handled the passage of time differently from its counterparts. I had my doubts about the dial's authenticity, but for the time being, it remained a strong contender.

The case in question grabbed my attention with its distinctive crown and serial number engraved between the lugs. Coupled with the faceted lugs, decagonal caseback, and stepped bezel, it screamed François Borgel, one of my favourite case makers.

We'll skip the Taubert & Fils dilemma—that's a story for another time.

When buying vintage, you've got to know what to look for. François Borgel was a renowned case maker who crafted some of the most recognizable, and earliest, waterproof cases. Many pieces featured the signature (Taubert) decagonal case, whereas later models, like this Mildo, sported round midcases and bezels featuring a decagonal caseback. Unlike Movado and P***k counterparts, the Mido cases didn't bear the FB mark. It adds a bit of "IYKYK" (as the kids say) to the pieces. An area where only those with a keen eye or a fanatical obsession know what they're looking at.

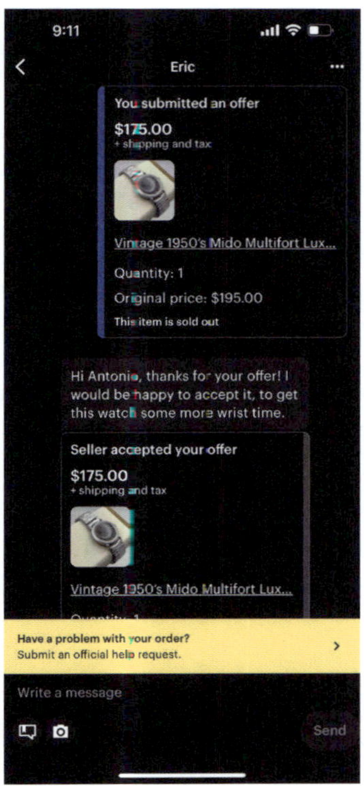

Look, I sell watches for a living, but this one isn't about profit. I'm in it for keeps.

The asking price was 195 USD, just over my budget, but the listing had a "Make Offer" option. If I didn't have a cache of extra straps and access to wholesale watch repair, I might have been inclined

to make an offer below my initial budget to compensate. These extras cost money and should always factor into any watch purchase. You wouldn't buy a bike with no wheels, would you? I will admit, in my rush, I did fuck up a little bit. I forgot about t a x e s. Don't be like me, when buying on a budget—ensure the final price includes all dues. But it was too late now. I'd already paid.

I realized a few years ago that although we all have "grails" or dream pieces, the watches we end up wearing the most are the ones we love. When this piece came in, I was smitten. I loved the case, the size, the dial and its warm patina. After a few cosmetic touches, I wore the piece nonstop. When Baltimore's rainy days roll in, I switch to a slightly more water-resistant piece. But come sunshine, I break it out and enjoy the dial in the sunlight. My advice? Buy what you love, not what people tell you to buy.

61

Joel Laplace
@jojolamontre

As you know, I make it my mission not to miss a watch fair in Switzerland: Geneva, Zurich, L'Abbaye in the Vallée de Joux, and naturally, Aran-Villette in the Lavaux region. For our readers overseas, Lavaux is presented as a wine-growing region in the canton of Vaud, known for its terraced vineyards on the shores of Lake Geneva. On 28 June 2007, Lavaux was listed as a UNESCO World Heritage Site!

This is one of the tinier watch gatherings, with a cosy dozen exhibitors, but the location is one-of-a-kind. Picture snow-capped peaks, lush vineyards, and a breathtaking view over Lake Geneva. My routine is to chug along by train from Lausanne. Next stop: Villette! Then, it's a hearty climb to the communal hall that hosts this annual event at the close of March.

This year, my dealer friend, Mateusz, aka @thetimekee-per, made the jaunt over from London. We caught up with him and my friend Thery, aka @hicnunwatches, at the legendary 'Le Simplon' bar behind Lausanne station.

A boozy meal later, I couldn't let Mateusz get back to the hotel without giving him a taste of Lausanne's nightlife. We kicked off at the Bourg for an electronica gig, which, frankly, lacked the punch we were after. I then whisked him away to the Folklor club, but not before a pitstop at the famed student haunt, the Great Escape. On the eve of fairs, I steer clear of lively nights out since mornings can be merciless.

Somehow, I managed to herd Mateusz back to the hotel around 3 a.m.; we're sensible blokes, after all. I'll never forget that weekend in London at Mateusz's, where I missed my Sunday flight —but that's another story. I warned my sidekick that, for once, I wouldn't be up with

the larks for the fair and would catch up later in the morning. Waking up, I found Mateusz had vanished. No surprise there—he's always among the first to scout the stands. A trader later told me Mateusz still reeked of booze when he rocked up…

After circling the exhibitors about 15 times, we kicked back on the terrace, flaunted our finds, and polished off a few bottles of white wine. The sky was overcast, but the temperature was just right. There I met up with my Geneva pals, Harris @mendelwatches, Dahl Brunel, and my very first boss, Marco Gabella, founder of Watchonista and horological ashtray collector.

Come 3 p.m., we decided to roll back to Lausanne for a late lunch at the Grand Chêne brasserie, which is open all hours. During the meal, I sold the smallest chronograph ever made for a friend—the famed Valjoux 69, with a dial diameter of just 24 mm! As a token of thanks, Mateusz gifted me a smashing Olma boy-size in a Tre-Tacche case. Take a wild guess what language the numerals on the dial are in!

The aim of this write-up? The quest to nab a gem for the CHF 150 tossed my way by Maxime and Lorenzo, the masterminds behind heist-out. The bounty? None other than the chic Ebel ashtray, mirroring the design of the Sport Classic case, the brand's iconic model launched in 1977. You've guessed it —it's now part of… Marco Gabella's collection!

The Vuille Era of Rolex
By Brendan M. Cunningham PhD

Wristwatch provenance. It's that special something that elevates an auction lot to the cover of a catalogue. It electrifies bidding, leading to record results. Where does provenance come from? Hollywood? You bet. That Brando Explorer appreciated $4 million in a handful of years. Speed? Do doubt. Paul Newman's "DRIVE CAREFULLY ME" caseback engraving earned almost $6 million per word, and that was well before the pandemic run-up in prices. Outer space? Collectors are over the moon for it. Astronaut Dave Scott's Speedmaster went for more than $1.6 million all the way back in 2015.

The word provenance is an English language derivative of the French word "provenir", meaning "come or stem from." What's interesting is that watches with marketable provenance don't originally come from the source of that provenance. Sure, Paul Newman's Daytona went through his hands, but those were not the hands that made it. It's easy to name the brand that brought a watch into the world: it's right there on the dial. But outside indies, where maybe a single watchmaker like Dufour crafts the metal, we rarely know the person who was there at a watch's birth, that moment when the watchmaker places the balance on the mainplate and the ticking begins.

There's an exception, though. There are records of a watchmaker who spent time at Rolex early in the 20th century. Many escapements crossed this watchmaker's bench from 1929 to 1939. Given this watchmaker's many accomplishments, I'd suggest Rolexes from this era have a specific provenance that may not be as well-known as it should be.

The watchmaker in question is Louisa Vuille.

Vuille was born in Villeret, a town once home to Blancpain and Minerva. Famed automata specialist Pierre Jacquet-Droz was born in the same town. Vuille's father was a watchmaker. In an interview, Vuille pointed out that he was an "horloger complet," i.e., a "complete watchmaker." This meant he had mastered a wide range of skills, including parts manufacturing, assembly, and after-sales service. Vuille made it clear, though, that as a woman, she was not able to complete formal training as a complete watchmaker. Instead, women were limited to training in the skills required for the regulation of escapements. Such skills are necessary for obtaining timekeeping accuracy in each watch produced or serviced.

Just as women in numerous modern professions have been held back by a "glass ceiling," women in the early 20th-century watch industry faced an "escapement ceiling." Watchmaking schools would not formally train them in skills required to finish, say, or assemble a watch. Nevertheless, despite the limits of her possible opportunities at the bench, Vuille trained up to the limit and became adept at manipulating and adjusting the escapement. After her family moved to Geneva, Vuille's father taught her the full complement of skills acquired by "complete" watchmakers.

After several experiences in smaller workshops, in 1929, Vuille found employment in a Rolex atelier in the Passage du Terraillet, a neighbourhood in Geneva south of the Rhone River (Geneva's official web page describes this neighbourhood as a "district of old earthen utensil merchants"). There is no definitive information about exactly where Vuille worked in this neighbourhood. Still, there is a photograph taken by Charles-Eduard Boesch showing a multi-story building with a large vertical Rolex sign at Rue De March 8-14, roughly 60 meters down the street from the actual Passage du Terraillet (unfortunately, the photograph is not dated, but Boesch passed away in 1961, so the picture predates that year). While it could be that Vuille did not work in the building with a large Rolex sign in the Passage du Terraillet district, it seems more likely that she did.

For Rolex, the Vuille years were a time when precision in timekeeping was a high priority. There are reports that in 1935, the midpoint of Vuille's Rolex career, the brand submitted 500 Prince watches for chronometer-grade testing. All of them received an "Especially Good" rating (TimeZone: TZ Classics » The Kew A Rolex watches; what, why & how many?). Vuille's time at Rolex set the foundation for subsequently produced "Kew A" Rolexes, perhaps the most accurate watches the brand ever created (The Rolex Kew A: Quite Possibly (And Very Likely) The Most Accurate Rolex Ever Made - Hodinkee).

There are reasons to believe that Vuille generally showed a high level of skill as a watchmaker. When she asked to work part-time, her bosses agreed. It was during her employment at the Rolex atelier, though, that Vuille showed an interest in improving conditions for herself and others. She and her fellow watchmakers worked on the 4th floor of the Rolex building beneath a glass roof, likely there to provide more light so that watchmakers could see small parts and details. There was a downside, though: temperature control. The watchmakers were extremely hot in the summer, and in the winter, they were freezing. Vuille was particularly concerned with the welfare of watchmakers testing for case waterproofness. Working with water was likely a fairly unpleasant task in the depth of winter.

At some point, Vuille decided to bring her concerns to her trade union, FTMH (Fédération des travailleurs de la métallurgie et de l'horlogerie). During a conversation with her boss, she learned he had found out about the complaint, and it seems he suspected she was the source. She was soon asked to return to a full-time schedule, which she did not want to do. In 1939, she stopped working for Rolex.

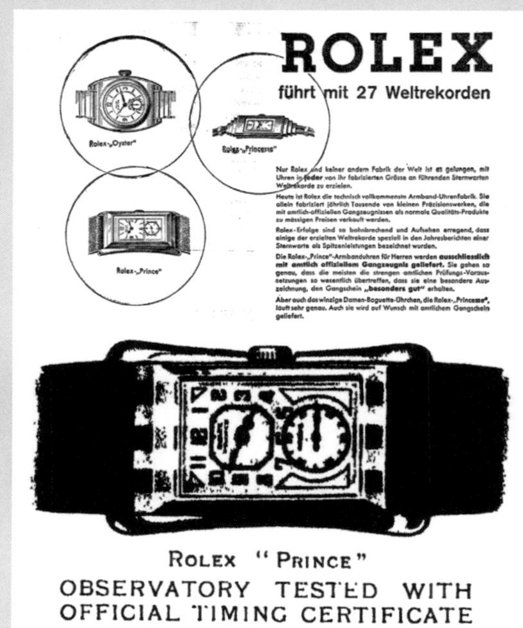
ROLEX
führt mit 27 Weltrekorden
Rolex-„Oyster"
Rolex-„Princesse"
Rolex-„Prince"
Nur Rolex und keiner andern Fabrik der Welt ist es gelungen, mit Uhren in jeder von ihr fabrizierten Grösse an führenden Sternwarten Weltrekorde zu erzielen.
Heute ist Rolex die technisch vollkommenste Armband-Uhrenfabrik. Sie allein fabriziert jährlich Tausende von kleinen Präzisionswerken, die mit amtlich-offiziellen Gangzeugnissen als normale Qualitäts-Produkte zu mässigen Preisen verkauft werden.
Rolex-Erfolge sind so bahnbrechend und Aufsehen erregend, dass einige der erzielten Weltrekorde speziell in den Jahresberichten einer Sternwarte als Spitzenleistungen bezeichnet wurden.
Die Rolex-„Prince"-Armbanduhren für Herren werden ausschliesslich mit amtlich offiziellem Gangzeugnis geliefert. Sie gehen so genau, dass die meisten die strengen amtlichen Prüfungs-Voraussetzungen so wesentlich übertreffen, dass sie eine besondere Auszeichnung, den Gangschein „besonders gut" erhalten.
Aber auch das winzige Damen-Baguette-Ührchen, die Rolex-„Princesse", läuft sehr genau. Auch sie wird auf Wunsch mit amtlichem Gangschein geliefert.
Rolex "Prince"
OBSERVATORY TESTED WITH
OFFICIAL TIMING CERTIFICATE

Soon after that, she relocated to Annemasse, France. Late that year, on September 9, 1939, France declared war on Germany. After Germany invaded France in 1940, Vuille bravely decided to fight against fascism, in her own way. As she put it, Vuille operated "a mailbox," transmitting letters as a member of the French Resistance's communications branch.

In 1943, Vuille moved back to Geneva. Her sister was expecting a child, and Vuille wanted to help with the newborn. She also continued working in watchmaking, joining (at different times) Niton (a movement manufacturer that supplied Tiffany's, Patek Philippe, Breguet, and A. Lange & Sohne), Reuge (a specialist in musical automata) and Chatelain (a watch and jewellery manufacturer now owned by Chanel).

During this time, Vuille continued her activism outside the watch industry. In 1946, she gave her first speech on a topic close to her heart. At that time, women did not have a guaranteed right to vote throughout Switzerland. On the Plaine de Plainpalais, she advocated for Swiss women's suffrage. Throughout her subsequent political career, Vuille worked fervently to secure Swiss women's access to the ballot box. In 1971, thanks to her efforts and many others, Swiss women earned equal voting rights.

There is no question that Vuille's accomplishments are worthy of celebration. You may be asking: what does any of this have to do with wristwatch provenance, the subject I began with? While we may not presently know of any watches owned by Vuille, we do know a period during which many Rolex watches passed across Vuille's bench in Geneva: 1929-39. Which Rolex watches are associated with this era?

One standout is the Rolex Prince reference 1862, particularly the chronometer-grade models. Many of these date to Vuille's time in Rolex's manufacture. Earning a chronometer rating requires a high degree of reliability and accuracy. Rolex would likely entrust regulation of such timepieces to those exceptionally skilled at manipulating a hairspring, such as Vuille.

The cushion-cased Rolex Oyster, reference 2081, is another design contemporary to Vuille. The Oyster was heavily advertised for its reliable waterproofness, and Vuille described tests for waterproofness during her time in Rolex's workshop.

Vuille would have also seen the emergence of automatic movements in Rolex's lineup when the brand introduced its "Perpetual" version of the Oyster. The earliest is reference 1858, dating to 1933. Automatically wound Rolexes from this era are sometimes called "Bubblebacks." Pieces that earned a chronometer rating were also more likely to have passed through Vuille's hands.

Conclusion

There is growing awareness of Louisa Vuille's importance in the history of Switzerland and watchmaking. In 2019, Rue de la Coulouvrenière, a larger thoroughfare just south of the Rhône River in Geneva, was given a second name: Rue Louisa Vuille. As part of a project named "100 Elles," a second street sign, in pink, was affixed with the street's alternate name below the traditional, blue Genevan street sign.

There are currently efforts underway to permanently name a stretch of road after Louisa Vuille in a neighbourhood northwest of Geneva's city centre. Watch designs frequently earn a nickname when famous people wear them, such as the Paul Newman Daytona or the Evil Nina Universal Geneve Compax. Typically, the only time a watchmaker's name is associated with a timepiece is when she, he or they start a brand: see Dufour and Journe. Maybe it is time to name an era of watches after an illustrious watchmaker who we know worked at the bench of a brand: the era of Vuille Rolexes.

The pink "second name" sign for Rue Louisa-Vuille as part of the "100 Elles" project in Geneva

The Untapped
Influence of Subversiveness:
Insights by Ethan Demeuse

Ethan Demeuse is a visionary creative who has meticulously sculpted her own captivating universe, centred around watches, and deeply influenced by vintage advertisements and editorials. She is the mastermind behind the compelling and curated @ Gemsbondgirl777 Instagram account, a portal that transports its followers to a bygone era where subversiveness danced with visual artistry. In today's world, the spirit of subversiveness has waned, lost amidst a sea of societal hypersensitivity. Sometimes for the right reasons but occasionally for the wrong ones too. Perhaps its profound significance and pivotal values have been overlooked or misunderstood. Challenging boundaries has always been a catalyst for innovation, empowering creatives to break free and unleash their artistic prowess. Even within the traditional realm of watchmaking, subversiveness has been instrumental. It has revitalized visual campaigns and editorials, introducing innovative designs and fresh concepts to breathe new life into the industry. We invited Ethan to curate vintage visuals that encapsulate the essence of subversiveness and creativity from a time seemingly irreplicable.

Photographer
Mathias Labie

DEBONAIR

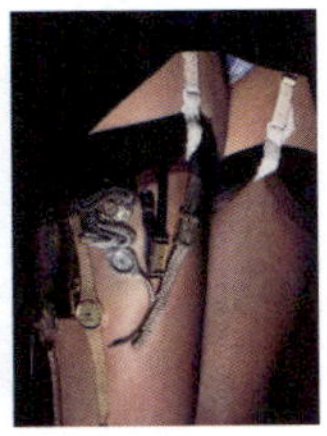

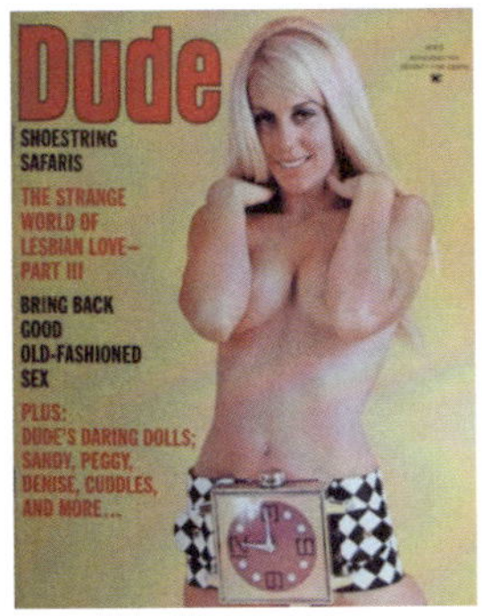
Dude
SHOESTRING SAFARIS
THE STRANGE WORLD OF LESBIAN LOVE— PART III
BRING BACK GOOD OLD-FASHIONED SEX
PLUS: DUDE'S DARING DOLLS; SANDY, PEGGY, DENISE, CUDDLES, AND MORE...

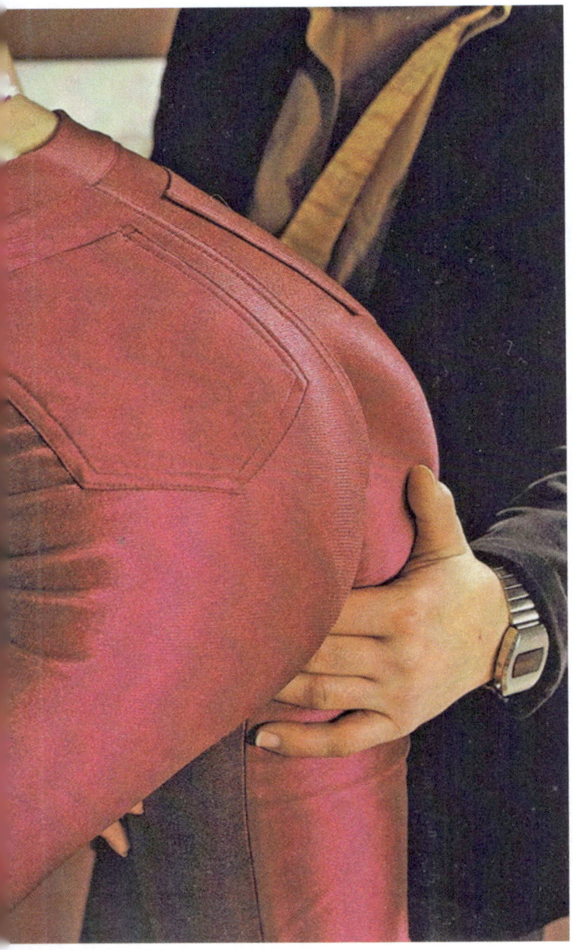

70

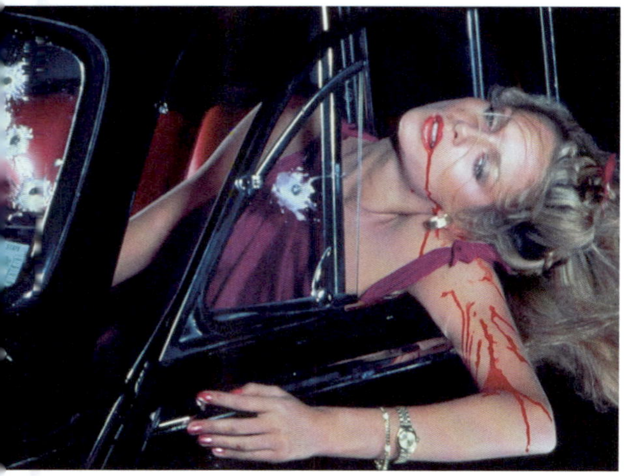

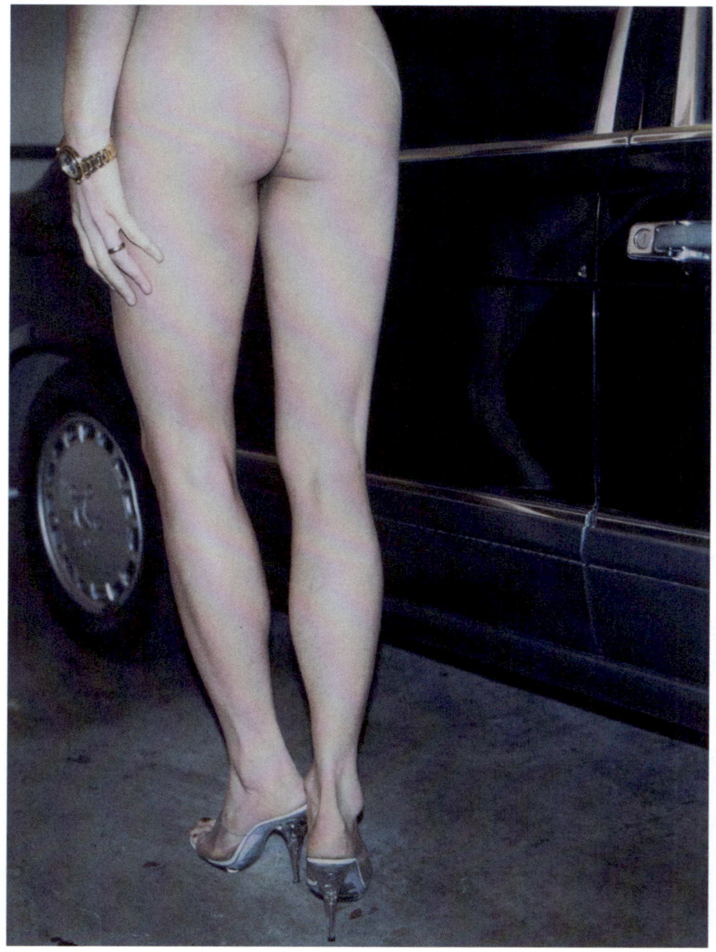

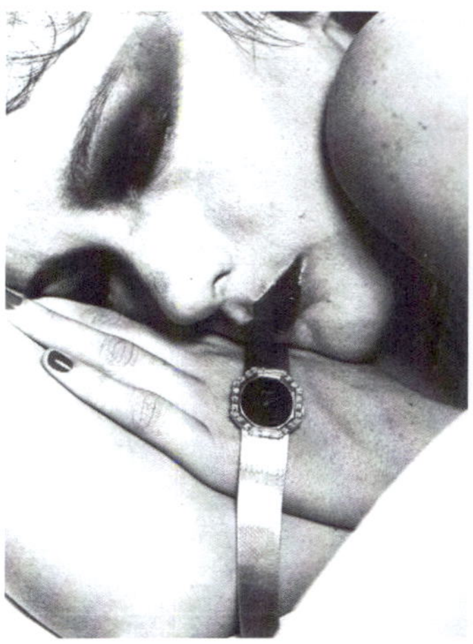

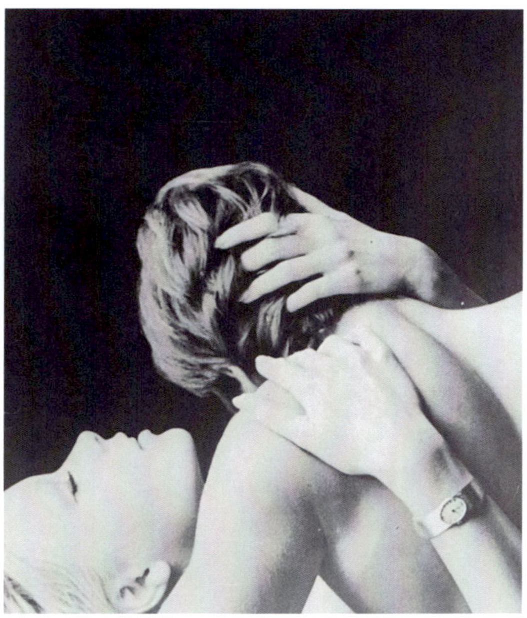

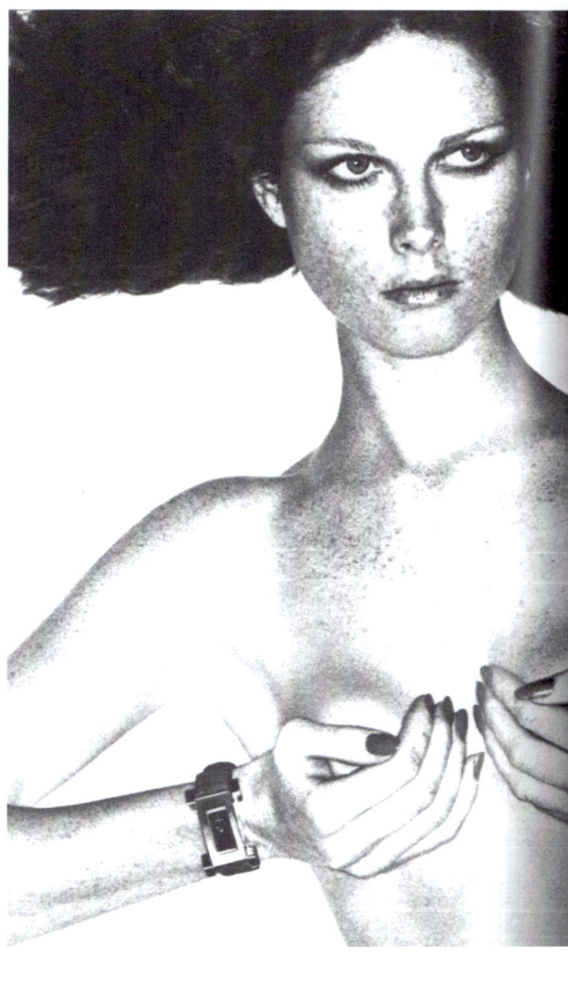

If you can identify the brand of each of these watches,
reach out to us—you might just unlock something special.

Métro Boulot Dodo

Makeup/hair
Manal El Bakkouchi
@manalelbak

Casting
Cécilia Manïkhouth
@ceciliamk

Stylist
Benjamin Georg
@bnjmn.mn

Models
Anne-Ly Roudil @ly_roudil
Zhe-hui Cao @zhe_huic
Toussaint Veux @touss_1

Felipe Barbosa @felipebarbosa.fr

Watches
N°1 @otottoi.watches
N°2 Tiffany & Co
N°3 @agm.1675
N°4 @lorenzo.maillard
N°5 @mendelwatches

JVC

Omega "Curb Chain"

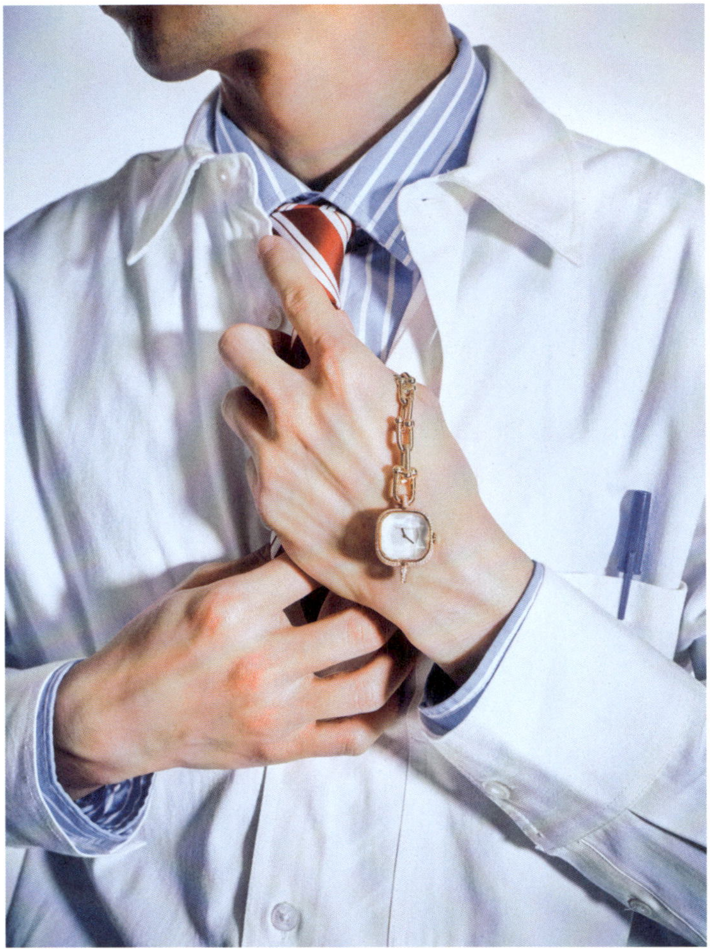

Tiffany & Co Hardwear Watch

Rolex Precision

Bel-Art

Corum Golden Bridge

The Return of Humility:
When Luxury Devours Its Own

Nicolas Amsellem

Photographer
Valentin Lam
@lamspics

Jaquet Droz & Leschot. These two names ignited my journey through horological history as I gradually uncovered the nebula lurking behind a brand that today prefers the shadow to the spotlight. In the 18th century, shoulder to shoulder with Breguet or Recordon, Jaquet Droz & Leschot spearheaded significant horological advancements, propelling Swiss watchmaking to global prominence. Pierre Jaquet Droz, a master of clock movements and an automaton virtuoso, surrounded himself with the finest artisans in Paris to clothe his art. His journey to Spain's royal court was a spectacle: with exquisite clocks delicately mounted on a vehicle crafted for the journey, it took him nearly two months to reach Madrid, traversing cities and the Pyrenees with his father-in-law and one of his craftsmen. After waiting months due to the royal couple's ailments, his mastery over metal expansion, chimes, and automatons captivated King Ferdinand VI and his wife, Marie-Barbara of Braganza. Without delay, Pierre Jaquet Droz returned to his lands, his pockets heavy with the sales of his exceptional clocks and automatons to members of the Spanish court. His partnership with two brilliant minds—his son and his neighbour's son, Jean-Frédéric Leschot—forecast a bright future as golden as their gears. Jaquet Droz & Leschot was born. Their timepieces, notably some extraordinary pocket watches, gained acclaim across courts across Europe and even as far as China through the prominent trading company James Cox London. Building their success on their oldest production site in La Chaux-de-Fonds, they established their atelier in Geneva in 1784, becoming the first modern watchmaking enterprise. Here, collaboration flourished—from diverse artisans to esteemed subcontractors—and Pierre Jaquet Droz's role in the Society of Arts championed the protection and education of the artistic trades.

This brief history serves to explain one thing: While the name Jaquet Droz & Leschot seldom graces our ears, this now-defunct enterprise, surviving only within Swatch Group as Jacquet Droz, boasts an extraordinary and tangible history. Their human saga, tied to the era's zenith, bestowed a legacy that even permeated Breguet's revered work on the 'perpétuelle'—the self-winding watch. Here lies a true cornerstone of our horological heritage.

"Since the 2nd century BC, [insert watch brand here] offers the world's most luxurious and innovative timepieces." Without lampooning the 'ancient' past of contemporary luxury watch brands, this is almost the kind of refrain you'll come across in their brochures and presentations. Yet where's the modesty and transparency they advocate? When it comes to history and innovation, they seem reluctant to put their principles into practice. Instead, most luxury brands often dredge up an ancient ancestor tied to horology as their genesis point.

Indeed, some brands tout increasingly ancient lineages, yet none of the works from these so-called ancestors has made it to posterity. The convenience of plucking a common 18th-century name to bestow legitimacy on a 21st-century 'luxury' watch clashes with dubious narrative leaps and, frankly, unnecessary ones. Why not embrace a more recent origin, mentioning only snippets of the past? The frenzy for the oldest Maison has faded. What people appreciate today are palpable legacies. When a brand can substantiate a tangible story, this always adds value, especially if it has retained its essence.

Today, in 2024, too many traditional 'luxury' brands have veered into misleading marketing, often false or at best 'flaux' —a hybrid of fake and vague.

They neglect the past while paradoxically harping on it with every presentation or mention of the brand. Enthusiasts, customers, and collectors expect a bit more consideration from these brands, especially given that most of horology's grand successes and achievements are behind us, and the future scarcely stirs excitement.

However, surveying the chronological landscape, it feels as if we're at the tail end of the odyssey—beyond the simple quest for precision, but also in terms of complications, water resistance, and the reliability of self-winding mechanisms. Yet, many watch brands tend to promote an era rife with superlatives but devoid of any humility.

Here, I'd like to revisit some ingenious milestones that, in my opinion, should allow us to view our current watches through a completely different lens, exposing the hollow narratives and propositions of some of today's brands. For practical reasons and to avoid straying too far from wristwatches, I've limited my focus to mechanical horology.

The pleasure of wearing timepieces, from simple to elaborate, owes not just to contemporary watchmaking manufacturers but to horology's natural evolution that slid beauties onto our wrists. I hold dear the episode in horology concerning the development of self-winding or 'perpetual' watches, which were extensively advanced by Jaquet Droz & Leschot. Without getting bogged down in details, some brands have overzealously claimed credit for this invention.

Beyond the myth of a 16th-century Jesuit creator, it's hard to pinpoint the originator of the self-winding watch. Yet the remaining archives and correspondence bestow credit to Abraham-Louis Perrelet for laying the ground-

work, in the mid-1770s, of this perpetual watch powered by the wearer's movements. Notable figures like Louis Recordon and Abraham-Louis Breguet, familiar with Perrelet's craft, pushed the invention further, though sadly, we do not have access to part of their work, which was typically unsigned. Recordon, a Swiss who established a part of his trade in London, was the first to patent an oscillating weight in 1780.

He essentially improved the spring's winding efficiency and reliability based on Perrelet's foundational work. Breguet, who had been working on the same mechanism in the 1770s, advanced further with innovations such as the oscillating weight with two going-barrels in tandem. We take it for granted now, but it required inventive genius to make a reliable self-winding mechanism: how could the oscillating weight be restrained once fully wound to prevent damaging the calibre? How could you wind a powerful mainspring with a weight? Breguet provided solutions, ensuring these perpetual timekeepers ended up in the pockets and palaces of the courts of Europe and beyond.

This early case exemplifies that the 'automatic' watch mechanism, which seems 'simple' today, was not born without trial and tribulation. The ingenuity of a few renowned watchmakers contributed to its evolution. Leading figures such as L. Leroy & Cie and the understated Léon Hatot endeavoured to refine the automatic winding system for wristwatches. All this groundwork was laid so that today, some oddballs may whimsically shake their watch and delight in seeing the seconds hand spring to life.

Indeed, the seemingly simple oscillating weight found in today's affordable Japanese watches or high-end horological pieces is the fruit of decades of significant work carried forward by a lineage of master watchmakers.

Around the same time, another indispensable work of genius—Abraham-Louis Breguet's brainchild —came to life: the tourbillon.

His invention stemmed from a simple observation: the lack of change in the balance wheel's position led to significant precision discrepancies. The reason? Earth's gravity and the unbalanced centre of gravity of the stationary balance wheel, positioned vertically in one's pocket. But in the late 18th century, was the solution for wearers to change the position of their pocket watch every hour? The idea was totally impractical. Breguet's solution was ingenious: his idea was to have the balance wheel move within a rotating cage (the tourbillon)—initially a one-minute rotation—to distribute friction and negate positional errors, thus averaging out the inconsistencies. The term 'tourbillon' harks back to a bygone definition, describing either a planetary system's rotation around a single axis or the force orbiting planets around the sun. The delightful invention spurred further iterations by watchmakers striving for reliability or cost-effective alternatives, rotating the entire movement in the watch rather than just the oscillator.

I won't keep you in suspense: today, the tourbillon is but an aesthetic flourish. A simple calibre, fine-tuned by artists, a.k.a precision timers, who were particularly active in the second half of the 20th century, easily surpasses a tourbillon's performance. Where some watch brands today want to make the tourbillon seem more than it is, the last century mainly succeeded in miniaturising it for our wrists but without further innovation.

Let's now leap back, counterintuitively, to a fundamental, 'elementary' horological endeavour compared to perpetual watches and the tourbillon—the pursuit of precision. The historical quest of horology, especially more recently with mechanical watchmaking, has always centred on precision. How can an object, through the interplay of forces and a network of wheels, accurately relay a day's hours, quarters, minutes, and seconds? That's our extraordinary fortune in 2024—to step back and view the entire timeline from a distance, from rudimentary timekeepers like the Astrolabe, the Nocturlabe, or hydraulic clocks, to weight-driven and precision pendulum clocks, followed by pocket watches, and finally, the wristwatches we cherish today.

I salute the generations of watchmaking artists devoted to this quest for precision, which shines not only in their mastery of the movement's power delivery but also in the exquisite craftsmanship of escapements. Hundreds of escapements have been conceived, yet only a handful of foundational types exist. I particularly recall George Graham's work on pendulums and clocks in the first half of the 18th century. He solved the issue of recoil that caused a loss of precision in early lever escapements and thus succeeded in having his creations featured on the most exceptional pieces, notably precision regulator clocks.

The 18th century even saw the use of a 'remontoir d'égalité' mechanism, also known as a 'constant device'. But what is that, you ask? It's a mechanism that sits between the power source (the mainspring) and the regulator (which dictates precision), ensuring constant intensity impulses. This system acts as a secondary power source, intermittently drawing energy from the mainspring and distributing it evenly to the regulator. This guarantees a steady power flow to the regulator while containing the energy from the mainspring. Pairing a refined escapement with a winding mechanism can catapult a

watchmaker to stardom. This is where the last few decades have brought some innovations. While Thomas Mudge's mid-18th-century lever escapement has become a mainstay in modern timepieces, watchmakers like Philippe René Jaccard with his 'Shockless' escapement and later George Daniels with his renowned Co-Axial have continued the storied tradition of escapement innovation, aiming to minimise friction and achieve a balance wheel's isochronism.

Perpetual watches, tourbillons, escapements—the bedrock innovations of watchmaking have existed for centuries within our mechanical marvels. The 20th century saw the culmination of horology's miniaturisation and the birth of exceptional designs and watches, exemplified by dial artistry and the use of precious materials. Why am I bothered to say this? Because it seems a grain of sand has wedged itself within the gears of our holy calibre.

Today, we should be more concerned about the fading of traditional watchmaking professions and the increasing scarcity of genuine innovation-oriented research. Not another run-of-the-mill unveiling of some Titanium Tech Hardcore watch case, but the pioneering spirit that inspired watchmakers to concoct countless—and often useless— escapements, propelling their craft forward. Watch brands should take a step back. Beyond graphical novelties and sparse faux breakthroughs, they've invented little in our age. It's okay to boast, but only when presenting a genuinely innovative timepiece.

Perhaps the diminished need for precise timekeeping has spurred a creative ennui. When a farmer needed precise time to orchestrate his day, when a noble, bored at the opera, could discreetly check the time by feeling his tact watch in his pocket, when a WWI soldier could still consider himself alive by merely knowing the hour, or even when a diver tracked his diving times, watchmaking was a battleground. People fought to own a watch.

Today, we're often served the same old dish with a new garnish. What will it take to rekindle watchmaking's innovative spirit? Watchmaking advancements have always stemmed from the scientific minds of brilliant watchmakers. That's why we should look to the independents, the scientists, not the established brands and conglomerates, to 'reinvent the wheel.' For me, it's a piece's unique design or its eccentricity that speaks volumes!

What's Next
Daringly Designed Watches
by Matteo Violet Vianello
@matteo.vv

Interest in watches is soaring, with more voices, perspectives, and tastes than ever before. This expanding community is reshaping and broadening the notion of what a watch should be, how it should be worn, and by whom.

Gone are the days when dress watches were relegated to specific occasions, to be paired with only certain attire. The lines between masculine and feminine watch designs are fading, dissolving into a unified vision. Even the very concept of the watch as an object of design is in flux. For some, this represents a dilution of the traditions that drew them to horology in the first place. For others, it's a thrilling evolution. From my point of view, this tension is part of the fun.

The burgeoning appetite for uniquely shaped watches exemplifies this shift. People are increasingly captivated by designs that defy the notion that watches should be round, rectangular, or a variation of these two shapes. They're coming to appreciate that timepieces can be far more sculptural and adventurous than what is typically imagined.

The escalating allure of daringly designed Cartier pieces, such as the Crash, Pebble, or Bamboo, is a clear indicator of this trend. Although partially fuelled by the hype machine, I believe we're seeing a more enduring shift that will be here to stay. People will always seek designs that break the mould, allowing them to tell the world something about themselves.

Among my favourite designers in this avant-garde league are Andrew Grima, Gilbert Albert, and Pierre Cardin. It's telling that none of these individuals are watchmakers — two are jewellers, and one a fashion maestro. Unfettered by watchmaking norms, they craft with unbridled creativity.

Pierre Cardin's 'Espace' Collection, birthed in collaboration with Jaeger in the early '70s, echoes his overarching design philosophy. He sought to break the visual conventions of his era by combining basic geometric shapes, bright colours, and experimental materials. This approach was the hallmark of his work, from the futuristic space-age suits he designed for the Beatles to his dramatic furniture.

This conviction — that watchmaking can transcend to realms more experimental, adventurous, and daring than its current confines — inspired me to create Anoma. We aim to create uniquely shaped watches that defy the dogmas of watchmaking — hence our name, Anoma, which is short for anomaly.

We're inspired by bold individuals from within and outside the world of watches, from architect Charlotte Perriand to sculptor Constantin Brâncuși. They remind us that design is a frontier to be pushed, a medium through which to express our individuality. This June 2024, we will unveil our inaugural opus, the Anoma A1.

Biography—Matteo Violet Vianello

Based in London, Matteo is the Founder and Creative Director of Anoma, a brand focused on sculptural watchmaking. He previously worked at Sotheby's and was one of the first employees at A Collected Man, a leading platform for rare watches. He is an Academy Member of the GPHG.

93

94

Unmistakable

Golden Ellipse and 18 kt. blue colored gold. They invariably identify Patek Philippe designs. They tell you that the watch was finished entirely by hand, in the manner practiced by Patek Philippe since 1839. The Golden Ellipse was derived by Patek Philippe from the Golden Section, the principle

which already inspired t
of the Parthenon. The blu
colored gold of the dial is
of alchemy signed Patek

Diamond-set ladies' moc
4382). Gents' bracelet watch (Re
Also featuring the Golden Ellipse
colored gold are the cufflinks an

What's Next
By Ken Koshiyama
@kenkoshiyama

The watch I'm sporting today epitomises the trajectory of a particular market demand, albeit still a bit niche. If I were to draw out a category, it would be the so-called 'cocktail watches' adorned with metal bracelets. Pinpointing a specific era would be limiting; instead, I'd highlight a product philosophy: elegantly designed watches that break from convention yet remain easy to don for the everyday. Yellow gold is making a noticeable comeback, but every metal bracelet deserves the limelight. The Piaget Polo reissue or the recent surge in popularity of the Cartier Tank with link bracelets come to mind. Several factors account for this renaissance, but here are the top four:

The Market Trend
When I first entered the horology scene, Hublot's Big Bang had just made its splash—it was the era of large watches. I even bought a JLC Reverso Squadra myself. Back then, that was the vibe the market and my peers were riding. It's wild because, nowadays, I'd never buy that—far too bulky! I'd say the market is edging this way: watch cases are shrinking in size. Plus, people are embracing a more unisex approach to watches. Models that were once deemed feminine are now finding a new, eager male audience ready to 'dig' them.

Philosophy of the New Consumers
Veteran watch enthusiasts might be hesitant to venture into new territories, often sticking to more status-driven pieces with tried-and-tested designs like the Nautilus or the Royal Oak. The new guard, however, boasts a more pronounced and eclectic taste, seeking out the unusual. This mirrors the fashion industry, where contemporary buyers hunt for sharp, vintage pieces to stand out from the crowd on the subway. They're doing the same with watches, driving demand for these distinct timepieces. They're rarer, bolder watches, thus more reflective of their individuality.

Value Proposition
Since this category of watches is on the fringe, you can snap them up at accessible prices, and they pack a higher intrinsic value. They require unique craftsmanship and substantial production time—aspects increasingly valued by consumers. They're also scarcer due to the limited quantity produced back in the day, but also because of the number of pieces still in existence. Take the Audemars Piguet Bamboo or the Cobra—both stunning pieces from AP with unique designs and incredible finishes for their current price point. The Patek Philippe Ellipse, with its variety of bracelet options, springs to mind as another instance.

New Influencers, New Players
"heist-out" or the dealer Mendel Watches, to name just a couple, are spearheading the push for this type of watch. They utilise distinct communication styles and media, reaching a different breed of consumer. Thus, timepieces that may have fallen into oblivion are finding themselves back in the limelight.

At Chopard, where I work, the archives brim with models that align perfectly with the ethos of these pieces. The watch I'm wearing today, as well as the Ice Cube and our emblematic Happy Diamonds—initially designed for men, let's not forget—are all brimming with potential when we talk about this kind of horology. The first, with its Onyx dial and gold bracelet, holds considerable promise within this watch genre.

Biography—Ken Koshiyama

Based in Geneva, Ken Koshiyama formed his taste with the streetwear culture of Harajuku and the Berlin underground. Trained as a watchmaker, he apprenticed with Patek Philippe, and is now an haute horlogerie expert with Chopard. Before joining the Swiss watchmaker and jeweller, he began his career at BNB Concept, then worked alongside Emmanuel Emch at Romain Jérome.

A special thank you to

Nour Karam, Sophie Satorre, Laura Marino & Sophie Van Houten from Audemars Piguet, Jerôme Burgert & Gabriel Vachette from Serica, Florian Le bouhec, Dahl Brunel, Mathias Gratry & Nicolas Godel from GRAGO, Aurélie Streit & Pascal Ravessoud from FHH, Andrea Furlan & Laure Michel from Furlan Marri, Balthasar De Pury, Claude Alain Bugnon, Basile & Tristan Deschamps, Alessandro Fanciulli, Alain Borgeaud, Anne-Sophie Mallard, Aurélie Ménétrier, Emmanuel Gueit, Amélie Boeraeve, Léa Bruneau, Sunflowerman, Matteo Maillard, Xhevdet Rexhepi, Teresa Fini, Laureat Bakolli, Gianfranco Ritschel, Joel Laplace, Antonio Vespoint, Brendan M. Cunningham, Ethan Demeuse, Felipe Barbosa, Benjamin Georg, Nicolas Amsellem, Matteo Violet Viannello, Ken Koshiyama, Kelly de Geer.

9

The magazine owes its existence to the genius and extremist graphic designer, Valentin Vitus. Without him, it simply wouldn't exist. Rémi Le Plomb and Paul Chevalier for their dedication and support throughout the project. Emmanuel de Montbron for proofreading and translating this mag with passion. Guillaume Ferrand for this one-of-a-kind poster artwork. A huge asscheek kiss to all our CheniboyZ for their support, humour and creativity. Harris Skandalakis, Joel Laplace, Alessandro Fanciulli, Arthur Pfister, Thery Couturier, Nicolas Amsellem, Dahl Brunel, Julien Bon, Yoni Krissi, Antonio Vespoint and Scarlett Baker our one and only CheniGirl. To Barbara Sampaio for her unconditional love, patience, and support <3 Lorenzo Maillard. To Pauline, without you there is no me, no magazine. To Georgia, I've been wearing our little bracelet all along I promise <3 Maxime Couturier.